THE GOSPEL PROJECT FOR KIDS®

Table of Contents

↑

Write th

D1607197

The Gospel Project for Kids
Younger Kids Leader Guide

Volume 10

The Mission Begins

© 2020 LifeWay Press®

Ben Mandrell
President and CEO

Ed Stetzer
Founding Editor

Trevin Wax
General Editor

Brian Dembowczyk
Managing Editor

Landry Holmes
Manager, Kids Ministry Publishing

Jana Magruder
Director, Kids Ministry

Send questions/comments by email to
brian.dembowczyk@lifeway.com, or mail to

Managing Editor
The Gospel Project for Kids
One LifeWay Plaza
Nashville, TN 37234-0172

Or make comments on the Web at
www.lifeway.com

ISBN: 978-1-5359-8010-4
Item 005819523

Printed in the United States of America

Bible Study at a Glance

LEADER BIBLE STUDY
Familiarize yourself with the content and context of the Bible story and how it relates to God's plan of redemption

Preparation
Pray for your kids and contact families during the week. Gather and prepare session materials.

- Pray for your kids
- Send a parent email
- Print/download printables
- Assemble supplies
- Prepare videos

Introduce the Story
Build relationships with kids and introduce the day's Bible story through engaging activities.

- Opening Activities
- Activity Page

Say what?
Use the suggested "Say" dialogue to easily move between segments.

Teach the Story
Communicate the day's Bible story and discover God's big story.

- Big Picture Question
- Giant Timeline
- Bible Story

- Missions Moment
- Key Passage
- Sing

Younger Kids Leader Guide

Apply the Story

Reinforce the Bible story for multiple learning styles and lead kids to apply what they learned as they take part in God's big story.

- Key Passage Activity
- Discussion & Bible Skills
- Closing Activities
- Journal & Prayer

Suggested times
The times provided allow you to complete the session plan in an hour and fifteen minutes. Lengthen or shorten the session as needed.

Missions Moment
Introduce kids to missions and encourage them to take the gospel to the nations with designated missions awareness activities.

Make it fit

Customize the session plan to fit the needs of your church or classroom.

👤👤👤👤👤 Small Group Option

1) Kids arrive in small group rooms for "Introduce the Story." Welcome and build relationships with kids, help them work the activity page, and complete one of the activity options together.
2) Transition to an area in your room designated as the "Teach the Story" area. Watch the Bible story video or tell the Bible story. Utilize elements that fit your space, resources, and schedule.
3) Move to another area of your room for "Apply the Story." Reinforce the story point and Christ connection. Help kids apply what they have learned. Dismiss kids according to your kids ministry policies and procedures.

👤👤👤👤 👤👤👤👤 Small Group and Large Group Option

1) Kids arrive in small group rooms for "Introduce the Story." Welcome and build relationships with kids, help them work the activity page, and then complete one activity option together.
2) Use the countdown video or other transition to move to the large group room. Join the other small groups for "Teach the Story." Watch the Bible story video or tell the Bible story. Utilize elements that fit your space, resources, and time constraints.
3) Return to small group rooms to "Apply the Story." Reinforce the Bible story's story point and Christ connection. Dismiss kids according to your kids ministry policies and procedures.

Unit 28: The Holy Spirit Empowers

Unit Description:

After Jesus returned to heaven, the Holy Spirit—whom He had promised to send—was given to the disciples. Filled with the Holy Spirit's power, the small group of disciples shared the gospel boldly and the early church grew rapidly.

Key Passage:

2 Peter 1:3

Big Picture Question:

How does the Holy Spirit help Christians? The Holy Spirit comforts us, shows us our sin, and guides us as we live for God's glory.

Session 1:

The Holy Spirit Came

Acts 2

Story Point: God kept His promise to send the Holy Spirit.

Session 2:

Peter Healed a Man

Act 3–4

Story Point: The Holy Spirit gave Peter power to heal a man.

Christmas:

Jesus Was Born

John 1

Story Point: Jesus came to bring us life.

Session 4:

Faithful in Hard Times

1 Peter 1–2

Story Point: Peter encouraged believers who faced persecution.

Session 5:

Living Like Jesus

2 Peter 1

Story Point: Peter instructed believers to live like Jesus.

Younger Kids Leader Guide

The Holy Spirit Came

God kept His promise to send the Holy Spirit.

Peter Healed a Man

The Holy Spirit gave Peter power to heal a man.

Jesus Was Born

Jesus came to bring us life.

Faithful in Hard Times

Peter encouraged believers who faced persecution.

Living Like Jesus

Peter instructed believers to live like Jesus.

Use Week of:

Unit 28 · Session 1
The Holy Spirit Came

BIBLE PASSAGE:
Acts 2

STORY POINT:
God kept His promise
to send the Holy Spirit.

KEY PASSAGE:
2 Peter 1:3

BIG PICTURE QUESTION:
How does the Holy Spirit help
Christians? The Holy Spirit comforts us,
shows us our sin, and guides us as we live
for God's glory.

INTRODUCE THE STORY
(10–15 MINUTES)
PAGE 10

→

TEACH THE STORY
(25–30 MINUTES)
PAGE 12

→

APPLY THE STORY
(25–30 MINUTES)
PAGE 18

Leaders, grow on the go! Listen to session-by-session training every week on
Ministry Grid, Apple Podcasts, Spotify, or LifeWay's Digital Pass:
ministrygrid.com/gospelproject | gospelproject.com/podcasts

LEADER Bible Study

Before Jesus ascended to heaven, He instructed the disciples to go to Jerusalem and wait. Jesus promised that the Holy Spirit would come upon them. So the disciples went back to Jerusalem, where they waited and prayed for 40 days.

The time came for the Jewish festival called Pentecost, or the Feast of Weeks. As with the Passover festival, Jews from all over the Roman Empire would be at the temple in Jerusalem.

During this festival, the Holy Spirit came to the disciples in Jerusalem. They heard a sound like a violent, rushing wind. When the Holy Spirit filled Jesus' followers, they were able to speak in foreign languages. They went out into the city and began to preach, and the Jews from all over the world were amazed. These men were from Galilee, but they were speaking in languages the visitors could understand.

Some of those who heard this thought the disciples were drunk. But Peter explained that God had kept His promise to send the Holy Spirit. He reminded them of the prophet Joel's words: "I will pour out my Spirit on all humanity" (Joel 2:28).

The disciples told about God's plan. The Holy Spirit convicted the crowd and they asked, "Brothers, what must we do?" Peter told them to repent and be baptized in the name of Jesus. That day, three thousand people received salvation!

With the Holy Spirit's help, Jesus' disciples could share the gospel with the entire world. (See Acts 1:8.) God gives the Holy Spirit to everyone who trusts in Jesus as Lord and Savior. As you teach kids, emphasize that the Holy Spirit gives us power to do God's work, and He changes us to be more like Jesus.

The BIBLE Story

The Holy Spirit Came
Acts 2

On the day of Pentecost, Jesus' disciples were gathered together in Jerusalem. All of a sudden, a sound came from heaven. It was like a strong rushing wind, and it filled the whole house where Jesus' disciples were staying. Then tongues appeared like flames of fire, and they rested on each of the disciples. The disciples were filled with the Holy Spirit, and the Holy Spirit gave them the ability to speak in languages they didn't even know!

Now, Jews were in Jerusalem who had come from every nation. They heard the disciples' voices in their own languages, and they were amazed! How could the men from Galilee speak so many languages?

Peter stood up and said, "I'll tell you what's happening." He reminded the people of something the prophet Joel had said long ago: "God says, 'I will pour out My Spirit on all people … I will show you wonders in the heavens above and signs on the earth below … Then everyone who calls on the name of the Lord will be saved.'"

Peter said, "You saw the miracles, wonders, and signs God did through Jesus. Even though God planned for Jesus to die, you used lawless people to nail Him to a cross and kill Him. **But death did not keep hold of Jesus; God raised Jesus from the dead.**"

Then Peter said, "You have seen the truth: **Jesus is alive! He went up to heaven to be with God the Father.** Do not doubt this." Peter continued, "When you killed Jesus, you killed the Messiah!"

The Holy Spirit convinced the people that Peter was telling the truth. "What must we do to be saved?" they asked.

Peter told the people to repent, to turn away from their sins and to turn to God. "God will forgive your sins, and you will receive the gift of the Holy Spirit. Be baptized in the name of Jesus," he said.

Everyone who believed Peter's message was baptized. That day, about three thousand people joined Jesus' followers. They learned what Jesus' disciples taught, and they met with other believers every day. They broke bread together and prayed.

Christ Connection: God kept His promise to send the Holy Spirit. With the Holy Spirit's help, Jesus' disciples could begin their work to share the gospel with the entire world. God gives the Holy Spirit to everyone who trusts in Jesus as Lord and Savior.

Bible Storytelling Tips

• **Use Language:** Practice saying a few phrases of the Bible Story in another language. When you reach the part of the story where the disciples are speaking other languages, repeat the phrases you practiced.

• **Use spacing:** Stand on one side of the stage while discussing the disciples in their lovked room. Move out of the "room" when the Holy Spirit comes. Stand amongst the kids while speaking about Peter's sermon.

INTRODUCE the Story

SESSION TITLE: The Holy Spirit Came

BIBLE PASSAGE: Acts 2

STORY POINT: God kept His promise to send the Holy Spirit.

KEY PASSAGE: 2 Peter 1:3

BIG PICTURE QUESTION: How does the Holy Spirit help Christians? The Holy Spirit comforts us, shows us our sin, and guides us as we live for God's glory.

Welcome time

Greet each kid as he or she arrives. Use this time to collect the offering, fill out attendance sheets, and help new kids connect to your group. Prompt kids to discuss a time they waited for something wonderful, such as a birthday party or a holiday celebration.

SAY • When we want something good, but it hasn't arrived yet, we have to wait. Waiting can feel very difficult, but it is often a part of our lives. Today we will learn about a time Jesus' disciples waited for something wonderful and what happened when that wonderful event finally happened.

Activity page (5 minutes)

· "Power Surge" activity page, 1 per kid
· pencils or markers

Invite kids to complete the "Power Surge" activity page. Kids will draw lines to match each item on the left with the source of that item's power.

SAY • Flashlights need batteries, cars need gas, and flowers need sunshine to do what they are made to do; people need the Holy Spirit to obey the commands God has given us! Today we will learn about the time the Holy Spirit came.

Session starter (10 minutes)

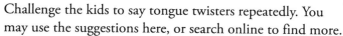

OPTION 1: Tongue Twisters

Challenge the kids to say tongue twisters repeatedly. You may use the suggestions here, or search online to find more.

- Goggles topple purple circles circling toppled cycles.
- Yellow bellied lizard gizzards bellow belly giggles.
- Red headed Beth bets beds against bird baths.

SAY • Today we will learn about the time the Holy Spirit arrived to Jesus' disciples. The Holy Spirit gave them the ability to speak languages they didn't even know! That's much more impressive than saying a tongue twister without jumbling the letters!

OPTION 2: Wind power

Invite the kids to form pairs. Give each kid a straw and hold a series of races where kids compete head to head to see who can blow their table tennis ball the farthest with a single breath.

· table tennis balls, 2
· drinking straws, 1 per kid

SAY • Wow, you all made some mighty wind with your breath and a straw. You blew those table tennis balls clear across the room! Today, we will learn about an even greater source of power that also has some things in common with wind! What power do you think that could be?

Transition to teach the story

TEACH the Story

SESSION TITLE: The Holy Spirit Came

BIBLE PASSAGE: Acts 2

STORY POINT: God kept His promise to send the Holy Spirit.

KEY PASSAGE: 2 Peter 1:3

BIG PICTURE QUESTION: How does the Holy Spirit help Christians? The Holy Spirit comforts us, shows us our sin, and guides us as we live for God's glory.

· room decorations
· Theme Background Slide (optional)

Suggested Theme Decorating Ideas: Decorate the room to look like a fire station. Place coiled hoses on a table. Spray paint 2-inch PVC pipes silver and set them up to look like firefighter poles. Consider contacting a local fire station to ask about borrowing some equipment for display.

Countdown

· countdown video

Show the countdown video as you transition to teach the story. Set it to end as the session begins.

Introduce the session (3 minutes)

· leader attire

[Leader enters wearing a firefighter costume.]

Tip: If you prefer not to use themed content or characters, adapt or omit this introduction.

LEADER • Hey there everyone! You may know just from looking at me, but I'm a firefighter. My job is to make sure any fires that start are put out quickly before they can damage too much or hurt anyone. It's dangerous work, but I really enjoy it. It makes me feel great knowing that I help people. And all this equipment definitely makes fighting fires safer nowadays than it was even a few years back!

One thing about firefighting equipment: it's not hard to recognize. I've never met someone who sees me in my gear who asks "so, what do you do for a living?" If you see me, you already know. In some ways, that's similar to believers. Our lives should look pretty different from anyone who doesn't believe the gospel. But we can't live that way on our own. We need to be equipped by God through the Holy Spirit! That reminds me of a Bible story. Let me share it with you.

Big picture question (1 minute)

LEADER • As we get into the story, I want you to think about this question: ***How does the Holy Spirit help Christians?*** I'll give you the answer later, but I want you to see if you can find some examples in the story of ways the Holy Spirit helps.

Giant timeline (1 minute)

Show the giant timeline. Point to individual Bible stories as you review.

· Giant Timeline

LEADER • If you have been coming week after week, you may remember that we recently discussed what happened near the end of Jesus' time on earth. Jesus died the death we deserve and rose from the grave on the third day. After that, Jesus spent time with His disciples for a little over a month before He ascended—rose up into the air—back to heaven to be with God.

But before Jesus left, He gave His disciples a mission, and a promise. The mission was to spread the gospel and make disciples who love and obey Jesus. The promise was for a Helper who would come to guide them in their mission. This week, we will learn about the time when the Helper finally arrived!

Tell the Bible story (10 minutes)

- Bibles
- "The Holy Spirit Came" video
- Big Picture Question Poster
- Bible Story Picture Poster
- Story Point Poster

Open your Bible to Acts 2. Use the Bible storytelling tips on the Bible story page to help you tell the story, or show the Bible story video "The Holy Spirit Came."

LEADER • Before the Holy Spirit came, Jesus' disciples were locked in a room, afraid of the religious leaders who had crucified Jesus. After the Holy Spirit, Jesus' disciples rushed out to begin boldly sharing about Jesus. Nothing about the disciples themselves had really changed. They didn't have a sudden burst of new knowledge or wisdom; what they had was the Holy Spirit in their lives!

The Holy Spirit gave the disciples boldness to proclaim the good news. He gave them wisdom to remember what Jesus had taught them. He even gave them power to speak in languages they had never studied or learned! He is the amazing fulfillment of Jesus' promise that God would be with believers forever.

The Holy Spirit is the third Person of the Trinity. That means He is fully God just as Jesus and the Father are fully God. He is the Helper Jesus promised to send. He lives with all believers and gives us the power we need to live for God's glory. *How does the Holy Spirit help Christians? The Holy Spirit comforts us, shows us our sin, and guides us as we live for God's glory.* Without the Holy Spirit, no one could love and obey God, and with Him anyone can have a huge impact to change the world for God's glory.

Christy connection

LEADER • **God kept His promise to send the Holy Spirit.**
With the Holy Spirit's help, Jesus' disciples could
begin their work to share the gospel with the entire
world. God gives the Holy Spirit to everyone who
trusts in Jesus as Lord and Savior.

Note: You may use
this opportunity to
use Scripture and
the guide provided
to explain how to
become a Christian.
Make sure kids
know when and
where they can ask
questions.

Questions from kids video (3 minutes)

Show the "Unit 28, Session 1" questions from kids video.
Prompt kids to think about how the Holy Spirit has
changed them. Guide them to discuss how they can know
they have the Holy Spirit with them.

· "Unit 28, Session 1"
Questions from Kids
video

Missions moment (3 minutes)

Play the "Lottie's Love" missions video.

LEADER • When the Holy Spirit filled Jesus' followers, they
were able to do so much more than they could with
their own power. Missionaries have the power of
the Holy Spirit, so they can make more followers of
Jesus. Lottie Moon was a missionary who served in
China over 100 years ago, but people still remember
her today. We can support missionaries—and even be
a part of sharing the gospel—so that we honor God
by obeying His plans for the world.

· "Lottie's Love"
missions video

Key passage (5 minutes)

Show the key passage poster. Lead the boys and girls to
read together 2 Peter 1:3. Then sing "Life and Godliness
(2 Peter 1:3)."

LEADER • There is no better source of power and guidance
than the Holy Spirit who lives within us. Peter wrote
this key passage as part of his letter to believers. He

· Key Passage Poster
· "Life and Godliness
(2 Peter 1:3)" song

wanted them to know that the Holy Spirit gives us everything we need to live for God.

Sing (4 minutes)

· "This is Where the Mission Begins" song

LEADER • Jesus left earth, but He did not leave us alone. We have the Holy Spirit in our lives to help us love and obey God. We are on mission for God!

Sing together "This is Where the Mission Begins."

Pray (2 minutes)

Invite kids to pray before dismissing to apply the story.

LEADER • Father, thank You for sending the Holy Spirit. Help us to listen to His voice and obey You in all we do. Give us courage to live on mission for You. Amen.

Dismiss to apply the story

The Gospel: God's Plan for Me

Ask kids if they have ever heard the word *gospel*. Clarify that the word *gospel* means "good news." It is the message about Christ, the kingdom of God, and salvation. Use the following guide to share the gospel with kids.

God rules. Explain to kids that the Bible tells us God created everything, and He is in charge of everything. Invite a volunteer to read Genesis 1:1 from the Bible. Read Revelation 4:11 or Colossians 1:16-17 aloud and explain what these verses mean.

We sinned. Tell kids that since the time of Adam and Eve, everyone has chosen to disobey God. (Romans 3:23) The Bible calls this sin. Because God is holy, God cannot be around sin. Sin separates us from God and deserves God's punishment of death. (Romans 6:23)

God provided. Choose a child to read John 3:16 aloud. Say that God sent His Son, Jesus, the perfect solution to our sin problem, to rescue us from the punishment we deserve. It's something we, as sinners, could never earn on our own. Jesus alone saves us. Read and explain Ephesians 2:8-9.

Jesus gives. Share with kids that Jesus lived a perfect life, died on the cross for our sins, and rose again. Because Jesus gave up His life for us, we can be welcomed into God's family for eternity. This is the best gift ever! Read Romans 5:8; 2 Corinthians 5:21; or 1 Peter 3:18.

We respond. Tell kids that they can respond to Jesus. Read Romans 10:9-10,13. Review these aspects of our response: Believe in your heart that Jesus alone saves you through what He's already done on the cross. Repent, turning from self and sin to Jesus. Tell God and others that your faith is in Jesus.

Offer to talk with any child who is interested in responding to Jesus. Provide *I'm a Christian Now!* for new Christians to take home and complete with their families.

APPLY the Story

SESSION TITLE: The Holy Spirit Came

BIBLE PASSAGE: Acts 2

STORY POINT: God kept His promise to send the Holy Spirit.

KEY PASSAGE: 2 Peter 1:3

BIG PICTURE QUESTION: How does the Holy Spirit help Christians? The Holy Spirit comforts us, shows us our sin, and guides us as we live for God's glory.

Key passage activity (5 minutes)

· Key Passage Poster

Work together with your group to develop hand motions to go with the verse. Consider researching some sign language words to help. Ensure the whole group knows the motions, then say the verse with the motions multiple times. You may use the suggested motions and word cues.

- Power—Motion as though grabbing your left bicep with your right hand.
- Life—Make an L-shape with the thumb and forefinger of each hand. Place your hands below your chest, with your forefingers pointed at each other. Move your hands up over your chest toward your collar.
- Knowledge—Use your left hand to point to your temple with four fingers.
- Glory—Clap your hands together before moving them apart, one upwards and the other down.

SAY • Peter wanted believers to know that God's power is enough for us. He gives us everything we need!

· Bibles, 1 per kid
· Story Point Poster
· Small Group Timeline and Map Set
(005802970, optional)

Discussion & Bible skills (10 minutes)

Distribute a Bible to each kid. Help them find Acts 2.

Younger Kids Leader Guide
Unit 28 • Session 1

Ask the following questions. Lead the group to discuss:

1. What did the disciples hear as the Holy Spirit came upon them? (*a sound like a rushing wind, Acts 2:2*)
2. What languages did the disciples preach the gospel in? (*many languages; each listener heard his own language, Acts 2:6*)
3. Which prophet did Peter quote to explain the miraculous events the Holy Spirit was causing? (*Joel, Acts 2:16-21*)
4. How can we receive the Holy Spirit? *Guide kids to think about the gospel and what it means to believe the gospel to be saved. Remind them that works cannot save us, and we must come to Jesus in faith. Help them see that all who repent and believe the gospel receive the Holy Spirit.*
5. How has the Holy Spirit affected your life? *Guide kids to talk about ways they have seen the Spirit working in their lives or the lives of their family members who are saved. Help them think through the kinds of traits God said would mark a believer, such as love, kindness, faithfulness, and so forth.*
6. Who can we tell about Jesus by the power of the Holy Spirit? *Explain that with the Spirit's power, we can tell everyone the gospel. Guide kids to think about specific people they can share the gospel with. Help them plan a time and a way to talk about Jesus, and encourage them to trust the Spirit for boldness.*

SAY • **God kept His promise to send the Holy Spirit.** God keeps all His promises. When we believe the gospel and have faith in Jesus, we are saved and the Holy Spirit fills us. He helps us live on mission for God.

Option: Retell or review the Bible story using the bolded text of the Bible story script.

Activity choice (10 minutes)

· "Chinese Characters"
  printable
· paper
· pencils

OPTION 1: Chinese characters

Display the "Chinese Characters" printable. Provide each kid with paper and a pencil. Encourage the kids to imagine they are in one of Lottie Moon's classes by practicing their writing and copying the Mandarin Chinese characters to their papers.

Tip: Use this activity option to reinforce the missions moment found in Teach the Story.

SAY • Lottie Moon lived in China from 1873 until her death in 1912. She worked as a missionary and teacher there. When she first arrived, few girls went to school, so she opened a school for them. She taught them many things, like writing and math, but most important of all, she taught them about Jesus. Who can we teach about Jesus in our lives?

LOW PREP

OPTION 2: Gospel sharing practice

Use "The Gospel: God's Plan for Me" (found on page 17) to guide kids through the gospel. Encourage them to practice sharing the gospel with one another to prepare for any opportunity they may have to share with a person who doesn't yet know Jesus. Consider using the following motions to help kids learn the phrases.

- God rules—Motion as though setting a crown on your head.
- We sinned—Use your forearms to make a large X over your chest.
- God provided—Rotate the X slightly so it looks like a cross.
- Jesus gives—Move cupped hands outward from belly as though giving a gift.
- We respond—Raise both hands into the air as in praise.

SAY • The gospel is the good news that Jesus died for our sin and rose again to defeat death. Everyone who responds to the gospel in faith will gain everlasting life. The gospel is too good to keep secret. When we love God and understand what He has done for us, the desire to tell others will grow inside us until we can't stay silent! With the Holy Spirit's power, we can tell the world about Jesus.

Reflection and prayer (5 minutes)

Distribute a sheet of paper to each child. Ask the kids to write about or draw a picture to answer the following questions:

- pencils and crayons
- paper
- Bible Story Coloring Page, 1 per kid

- What does this story teach me about God or about the gospel?
- What does this story teach me about myself?
- Whom can I tell about this story?

Make sure to send the sheets home with kids alongside the activity page so that parents can see what their kids have been learning.

If time remains, take prayer requests or allow kids to complete the Bible story coloring page provided with this session. Pray for your group.

Tip: Give parents this week's Big Picture Cards for Families to allow families to interact with the biblical content at home.

Unit 28 · Session 2
Peter Healed a Man

BIBLE PASSAGE:
Act 3–4

STORY POINT:
The Holy Spirit gave Peter power to heal a man.

KEY PASSAGE:
2 Peter 1:3

BIG PICTURE QUESTION:
How does the Holy Spirit help Christians? The Holy Spirit comforts us, shows us our sin, and guides us as we live for God's glory.

INTRODUCE THE STORY
(10–15 MINUTES)
PAGE 26

→

TEACH THE STORY
(25–30 MINUTES)
PAGE 28

→

APPLY THE STORY
(25–30 MINUTES)
PAGE 34

Leaders, grow on the go! Listen to session-by-session training every week on Ministry Grid, Apple Podcasts, Spotify, or LifeWay's Digital Pass: ministrygrid.com/gospelproject | gospelproject.com/podcasts

LEADER Bible Study

With the coming of the Holy Spirit at Pentecost, Jesus' disciples were empowered to carry out Jesus' mission for them: to take the gospel to all the nations. More and more people believed in Jesus. They met together at the temple to praise and worship God, and the first church began.

One afternoon, two of Jesus' disciples—Peter and John—went to the temple to pray. They encountered at the gate a man who could not walk. Rather than give the man money, Peter gave him something much more valuable: immediate physical healing in Jesus' name.

As you teach this Bible story to kids, keep three things in mind. First, Peter's healing the beggar was not magic; it was a miracle. Beginning in Acts 3:12, Peter responded to the people who were amazed at what had happened. "Why are you amazed at this … as though we had made him walk by our own power?" The man wasn't healed because Peter was a super-believer. Peter explained that it was by Jesus' power the man was healed.

Second, the man's healing made him happy and thankful. He entered the temple and rejoiced! Consider the wonderful miracle of salvation. We are dead in our sin, and God makes us alive in Christ! How we should rejoice and give thanks to the Lord!

Finally, Peter and John were bold in their witness. When confronted by the religious leaders, they did not shy away. Peter and John preached about the salvation found in Jesus. In fact, they said they were "unable to stop speaking about what [they had] seen and heard" (Acts 4:20).

The same power that enabled Peter to heal the man who was lame—the power of the Holy Spirit—enables believers today to live on mission for Jesus. Pray that God would give the kids you teach a willingness to be used by Him for His glory and for the fame of Jesus' name.

The **BIBLE** Story

Peter Healed a Man

Act 3–4

One afternoon, **Peter and John**—two of Jesus' followers—**went to the temple to pray. They saw a man sitting by a gate. The man could not walk.** Every day, the man's friends carried him to the temple. As people entered the temple, **the man asked them for money since he couldn't work.**

Peter said to the man, "Look at us." The man looked at Peter and John, expecting them to give him something.

Peter said, "I don't have any silver or gold for you, but I will give you what I do have." Then Peter said, "In the name of Jesus Christ of Nazareth, get up and walk!" Peter reached out and helped the man up. **All of a sudden, the man's feet and ankles were strong. He could walk!** In fact, the man leaped around! **He went into the temple with Peter and John, and he praised God. The people in the temple saw that the man was healed, and they were amazed.**

The next day, **the religious leaders asked** Peter and John, **"How did you heal this man?** By what power or in what name did you do this?"

Peter was filled with the Holy Spirit. He **said, "This man was**

24

Younger Kids Leader Guide
Unit 28 • Session 2

healed by the power of Jesus Christ from Nazareth. You nailed Jesus to a cross, but God raised Him from the dead. It is because of Him that this man is healed!"

Peter told the religious leaders that they rejected Jesus because they thought He was not important, but He is the most important One of all.

The religious leaders didn't know what to say. They **ordered Peter and John to never preach or teach in the name of Jesus again. Peter and John said,** "Do you think it would be right for us to listen to you instead of God? **We cannot be quiet. We must tell people about what we have seen and heard."**

Peter and John met with other believers and prayed that God would give them power to speak boldly and without fear.

Christ Connection: After Jesus returned to heaven, the Holy Spirit gave the disciples power to begin working. With the power of Jesus' name, Peter healed a man who was lame. Not even the religious leaders could stop Jesus' followers from sharing the good news about Jesus.

Bible Storytelling Tips

• **Act it out:** Invite kid volunteers to act out the events of the story as you tell it.
• **Use motion cues:** Start the story seated on the floor. When you arrive at the point where the man is healed, stand up and move about the stage with energy as you finish the story..

INTRODUCE the Story

SESSION TITLE: Peter Healed a Man

BIBLE PASSAGE: Act 3–4

STORY POINT: The Holy Spirit gave Peter power to heal a man.

KEY PASSAGE: 2 Peter 1:3

BIG PICTURE QUESTION: How does the Holy Spirit help Christians? The Holy Spirit comforts us, shows us our sin, and guides us as we live for God's glory.

Welcome time

Greet each kid as he or she arrives. Use this time to collect the offering, fill out attendance sheets, and help new kids connect to your group. Prompt kids to tell about the best gifts they have ever received.

SAY • On your birthday or certain holidays, you probably received gifts from your friends or family. Often though, the best gifts aren't toys, gadgets, or money. Today we will learn about a time Peter gave a wonderful gift to a man who asked for money.

Activity page (5 minutes)

· "Something Better" activity page, 1 per kid
· pencils or markers

Invite kids to complete the "Something Better" activity page. Instruct the kids to circle the item they think is better in each pair of items. Ask them to compare answers with one another.

SAY • We all have different preferences. Today, we will learn about a man who asked Peter for money. What do you think Peter gave him instead? We'll learn that it was something much better than money.

Session starter (10 minutes)

OPTION 1: Leapscotch

Use tape to make a modified hopscotch style grid on the floor. Make each square a few feet away from the next, so that kids must jump a bit further than they would in a normal hopscotch game. Then play a game of "leapscotch."

SAY • Normally this game has the squares much closer together and we call the game *hopscotch*. But today we had to leap to get from square to square. Today, we will learn about a time Peter healed a man who could not walk. Afterwards, the man was leaping around and praising God! How do you think Peter healed the man?

OPTION 2: Coin towers

Provide each kid with a few dozen pennies, nickels, or other coins. Give the kids time to sort, count, and stack the coins. Then challenge the kids to see how tall a tower they can build out of coins. Invite kids to work together to build something that won't easily fall over. When the kids are done with the coins, ensure they sanitize their hands.

SAY • Today we will hear a story about a man who could not walk. He would ask people to give him money because he could not work to earn money. When he asked Peter for money, he got something much better. What do you think Peter gave him?

Transition to teach the story

LOW PREP

· masking tape
· paper wad

Tip: You can search online to find hopscotch rules if you are unfamiliar with the game.

· various coins
· hand sanitizer

TEACH the Story

SESSION TITLE: Peter Healed a Man

BIBLE PASSAGE: Act 3–4

STORY POINT: The Holy Spirit gave Peter power to heal a man.

KEY PASSAGE: 2 Peter 1:3

BIG PICTURE QUESTION: How does the Holy Spirit help Christians? The Holy Spirit comforts us, shows us our sin, and guides us as we live for God's glory.

Countdown

· countdown video

Show the countdown video as you transition to teach the story. Set it to end as the session begins.

Introduce the session (3 minutes)

· leader attire

[Leader enters wearing a firefighter costume.]

Tip: If you prefer not to use themed content or characters, adapt or omit this introduction.

LEADER • Welcome back to the station, friends. For those of you who were not here last time, I'm firefighter *[your name]*. My primary job is to fight fires to prevent them from damaging people's property or hurting people. But firefighters respond to all kinds of emergency situations. Car accidents, chemical spills, natural disasters. There're all kinds of situations where we might be called.

But even though we firefighters can do a lot of things, there are some things we can't do. And a lot of things we can only do with help from the right equipment. For example we can only put our fires when we have the right equipment, like hoses, that help us transfer lots of water onto the fires we fight. And if someone were to be injured and paralyzed in an accident, we can probably save their life by rescuing them and getting them to a hospital, but there's nothing we can do to give a paralyzed person their ability to walk again. That's where our Bible story comes in.

Big picture question (1 minute)

LEADER • Last week we learned a new big picture question and answer. *How does the Holy Spirit help Christians? The Holy Spirit comforts us, shows us our sin, and guides us as we live for God's glory.* That means that when we repent of our sins and believe the gospel, the Holy Spirit lives within us to give us the power and wisdom we need to live on mission for God's glory. He helps us avoid temptation and say no to sin. He helps us remember God's love and goodness even in hard times. He even helps us remember and understand God's Word so we can obey it each day.

Giant timeline (1 minute)

Show the giant timeline. Point to individual Bible stories as you review.

· Giant Timeline

LEADER • Last week we learned that **God kept His promise to send the Holy Spirit**. Today, we're going to continue learning about the power of the Holy Spirit. Peter and John used the Holy Spirit's power to do something wonderful.

· Bibles
· "Peter Healed a Man" video
· Big Picture Question Poster
· Bible Story Picture Poster
· Story Point Poster

Tell the Bible story (10 minutes)

Open your Bible to Act 3–4. Use the Bible storytelling tips on the Bible story page to help you tell the story, or show the Bible story video "Peter Healed a Man."

The Holy Spirit Empowers

LEADER • I wonder what the man who was healed thought Peter was about to give him when Peter first said "I don't have money, but I'll give you what I do have." Maybe he thought he was about to get some food. Or maybe he thought Peter would give him some life advice. The Bible doesn't say. But the Bible does tell us how the man reacted after the healing.

The man immediately got up and began to jump, run, and praise God! In those days, a person who could not walk really couldn't work either. Things like wheelchairs didn't exist yet, so the man had little choice but to sit near the temple and beg for money to help him make ends meet. It's very likely that he felt hopeless much of the time.

When Peter healed him, Peter gave the man hope for his future. But Peter didn't heal the man by his own power or goodness. **The Holy Spirit gave Peter power to heal a man**. Peter used this miracle as an opportunity to tell others about Jesus. When people asked how the man had been healed, Peter was clear and confident in his reply. It was in the power and name of Jesus that the man had been healed.

More than that, Peter and John remained bold even when the religious leaders threatened them, had them arrested, and beat them. They knew that obeying God to preach the gospel was better than being comfortable or safe in this life.

Note: You may use this opportunity to use Scripture and the guide provided to explain how to become a Christian. Make sure kids know when and where they can ask questions.

Christ connection

LEADER • After Jesus returned to heaven, the Holy Spirit gave the disciples power to begin working. With the power of Jesus' name, Peter healed a man who was

lame. Not even the religious leaders could stop Jesus'
followers from sharing the good news about Jesus.

Questions from kids video (3 minutes)

Show the "Unit 28, Session 2" questions from kids video.
Prompt kids to think about times God's answers to our
prayers surprise us. Guide them to discuss how God uses all
things for His glory and our good.

· "Unit 28, Session 2"
Questions from Kids
video

Missions moment (3 minutes)

Measure 4 feet, 3 inches up from the floor and
mark that spot using a bit of tape on the wall. Print and cut
apart the "Lottie Moon Fact Strips" printable. Allow strong
readers to read the strips and then stand next to the height
marker on the wall. If time allows, let other kids compare
their height with the wall marker.

· measuring tape
· masking tape
· "Lottie Moon Fact
Strips" printabe
· scissors

LEADER • Lottie Moon was 4 feet, 3 inches tall, and she did
many great things in Jesus' name. She relied on the
Holy Spirit's power, not her own physical strength. In
Jesus' name, Peter healed a man who could not walk.
God gives people the power to serve other people in
His name. Anyone can do wonderful things with the
Holy Spirit's power in them.

Key passage (5 minutes)

Show the key passage poster. Lead the boys and girls to
read together 2 Peter 1:3. Then sing "Life and Godliness
(2 Peter 1:3)."

· Key Passage Poster
· "Life and Godliness
(2 Peter 1:3)" song

LEADER • Peter wrote these words to help believers know
that God gives us everything we need through the
Holy Spirit.

· "This is Where the
Mission Begins" song

Sing (4 minutes)

LEADER • Peter and John were bold because the Holy Spirit was filling them with power. They refused to stop talking about Jesus, no matter what. We have access to the same Holy Spirit, and thus the same power. We can live on mission for God!

Sing together "This is Where the Mission Begins."

Pray (2 minutes)

Invite kids to pray before dismissing to apply the story.

LEADER • Father, thank You for caring about our problems. Thank You that You heal us from our biggest problem, sin. Help us trust the guidance of the Holy Spirit and live our lives for Your glory. Amen.

Dismiss to apply the story

The Gospel: God's Plan for Me

Ask kids if they have ever heard the word *gospel*. Clarify that the word *gospel* means "good news." It is the message about Christ, the kingdom of God, and salvation. Use the following guide to share the gospel with kids.

God rules. Explain to kids that the Bible tells us God created everything, and He is in charge of everything. Invite a volunteer to read Genesis 1:1 from the Bible. Read Revelation 4:11 or Colossians 1:16-17 aloud and explain what these verses mean.

We sinned. Tell kids that since the time of Adam and Eve, everyone has chosen to disobey God. (Romans 3:23) The Bible calls this sin. Because God is holy, God cannot be around sin. Sin separates us from God and deserves God's punishment of death. (Romans 6:23)

God provided. Choose a child to read John 3:16 aloud. Say that God sent His Son, Jesus, the perfect solution to our sin problem, to rescue us from the punishment we deserve. It's something we, as sinners, could never earn on our own. Jesus alone saves us. Read and explain Ephesians 2:8-9.

Jesus gives. Share with kids that Jesus lived a perfect life, died on the cross for our sins, and rose again. Because Jesus gave up His life for us, we can be welcomed into God's family for eternity. This is the best gift ever! Read Romans 5:8; 2 Corinthians 5:21; or 1 Peter 3:18.

We respond. Tell kids that they can respond to Jesus. Read Romans 10:9-10,13. Review these aspects of our response: Believe in your heart that Jesus alone saves you through what He's already done on the cross. Repent, turning from self and sin to Jesus. Tell God and others that your faith is in Jesus.

Offer to talk with any child who is interested in responding to Jesus. Provide *I'm a Christian Now!* for new Christians to take home and complete with their families.

APPLY the Story

SESSION TITLE: Peter Healed a Man

BIBLE PASSAGE: Act 3–4

STORY POINT: The Holy Spirit gave Peter power to heal a man.

KEY PASSAGE: 2 Peter 1:3

BIG PICTURE QUESTION: How does the Holy Spirit help Christians? The Holy Spirit comforts us, shows us our sin, and guides us as we live for God's glory.

Key passage activity (5 minutes)

- Key Passage Poster
- "Key Passage Flip Cards" printable
- heavyweight paper
- scissors
- pens or pencils

Print the "Key Passage Flip Cards" printable double sided to heavyweight paper and cut apart. Provide one flip card to each kid. Challenge the kids to fold their flip cards to show only one level at a time. Kids will fill in the missing words on each level before flipping the card to work on the next level. Each level will have more words missing.

SAY • Peter wrote this letter to encourage believers who faced suffering because they loved Jesus. Peter wanted them to know that God gives us the power we need to honor Him with our lives.

When we put our faith in Jesus, God gives us access to the same power through the Holy Spirit. *How does the Holy Spirit help Christians? The Holy Spirit comforts us, shows us our sin, and guides us as we live for God's glory.*

Discussion & Bible skills (10 minutes)

- Bibles, 1 per kid
- Story Point Poster
- Small Group Timeline and Map Set (005802970, optional)

Distribute a Bible to each kid. Help them find Acts 3–4. Use the New Testament Israel Map to point out Jerusalem, where the story today took place. Ask the kids which division of the New Testament Acts is in. (*History*)

Ask the following questions. Lead the group to discuss:

Option: Retell or review the Bible story using the bolded text of the Bible story script.

1. What did the man who couldn't walk ask for? (*money, Acts 3:3*)
2. What did Peter do when people were gathered in amazement at the healing? (*preached the gospel, Acts 3:12-26*)
3. What did Peter and John do when ordered to stop talking about Jesus? (*refused to obey humans and chose to obey God, Acts 4:19*)
4. Will God heal every person who has an illness or disability? *Guide kids to think through two lenses: the lens of our physical lives now and our eternal lives with God. Even though not everyone will have their physical ailments healed now, everyone who believes in Jesus will one day live in a restored world with no pain, sadness, sickness, or death.*
5. Why was it OK for Peter and John to refuse to obey the authorities who arrested them? *Remind kids that the Bible contains many commands to obey leaders and submit to government authorities, but that God's authority always supersedes human authority. We obey human authorities as long as they do not command us to disobey God.*
6. When can we preach the gospel? *Guide kids to think beyond the simple answer of "all the time." Remind them that Peter used the opportunities in front of him to preach. We can preach all the time, and we can be strategic and plan specific ways to tell people about Jesus' work to save us.*

SAY • **The Holy Spirit gave Peter power to heal a man.** We have access to the same power through Jesus. God wants us to share the gospel boldly.

The Holy Spirit Empowers

· "Lottie's Tea Cake
Recipe" printable
· scissors
· pencils or pens
· tea cakes (optional)
· Allergy Alert
(optional)

Tip: Use this
activity option
to reinforce the
missions moment
found in Teach the
Story.

**LOW
PREP**

Activity choice (10 minutes)

 OPTION 1: Tea Cakes

Print enough copies of the "Lottie's Tea Cake Recipe" printables for each kid to take home one card after they are cut apart. Encourage the kids to write the name of a person they could make tea cakes for (or do another act of service to show love to). You may choose to make a batch of Lottie's Tea Cakes to bring in for the kids to taste.

SAY • When Lottie Moon first went to China, many children were afraid of her because she was not Chinese. She made tea cakes, which are like sugar cookies, and gave them to her neighbors so that they would get to know her. Over the years, she made thousands of tea cakes and told thousands of people about Jesus.

OPTION 2: Too many Simons

Select two or more volunteers to lead the game. Instruct the volunteers to give commands. The rest of the kids will only obey the commands of the volunteers when the volunteer says "Simon Says" before issuing the command. The kids may choose which of the two leaders' "Simon Says" commands they will obey.

SAY • That game was chaos, wasn't it? It's hard enough to only obey the "Simon says" commands when it's one leader giving them, but with many leaders and no clear direction on who you are supposed to obey, it's impossible to keep track of things.

In our story today, Peter and John had two different sets of commands: they had the commands of Jesus to share the gospel with everyone and heal people in His name; and the commands of the religious leaders to never speak about Jesus again. Thankfully, Peter and John were wise enough to know that Jesus is the most important leader to obey. He is God's Son!

The Bible tells us to obey government authorities, so we know that we don't get to live in ways that break the law. However, if anyone ever gives you a command that goes against Jesus, you can be sure that obeying Jesus is the right call, no matter who is asking you to disobey Him.

Reflection and prayer (5 minutes)

Distribute a sheet of paper to each child. Ask the kids to write about or draw a picture to answer the following questions:

- What does this story teach me about God or about the gospel?
- What does this story teach me about myself?
- Whom can I tell about this story?

Make sure to send the sheets home with kids alongside the activity page so that parents can see what their kids have been learning.

If time remains, take prayer requests or allow kids to complete the Bible story coloring page provided with this session. Pray for your group.

- pencils and crayons
- paper
- Bible Story Coloring Page, 1 per kid

Tip: Give parents this week's Big Picture Cards for Families to allow families to interact with the biblical content at home.

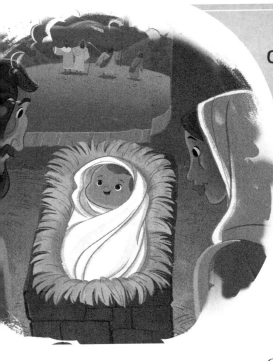

Christmas · Session 3
Jesus Was Born

BIBLE PASSAGE:
John 1

STORY POINT:
Jesus came to bring us life.

KEY PASSAGE:
2 Peter 1:3

BIG PICTURE QUESTION:
How does the Holy Spirit help Christians? The Holy Spirit comforts us, shows us our sin, and guides us as we live for God's glory.

INTRODUCE THE STORY
(10–15 MINUTES)
PAGE 42

TEACH THE STORY
(25–30 MINUTES)
PAGE 44

APPLY THE STORY
(25–30 MINUTES)
PAGE 50

Leaders, grow on the go! Listen to session-by-session training every week on Ministry Grid, Apple Podcasts, Spotify, or LifeWay's Digital Pass: ministrygrid.com/gospelproject | gospelproject.com/podcasts

LEADER Bible Study

God's plan all along was to send His Son into the world to save sinners. At just the right time, God the Son "emptied himself by assuming the form of a servant, taking on the likeness of humanity" (Phil. 2:7). The birth of Jesus was a miracle.

The Gospels of Matthew and Luke begin by giving details of the Messiah's birth: Mary became pregnant by the Holy Spirit and gave birth to a son. The baby was God's Son, and He had an earthly father—Joseph. As the angel had instructed, Joseph named the baby Jesus.

The apostle John began his Gospel in a different way. John 1:1 parallels the words of Genesis 1: "In the beginning ... " In the beginning, God spoke creation into existence. Everything was created through God the Son. (Col. 1:16) John names Jesus as "the Word." (John 1:3)

John 1 provides a bigger picture to accompany the story found in Luke 2:1-20. "The Word became flesh and dwelt among us" (John 1:14). As you teach kids about Jesus' birth, help them realize why Jesus came. Jesus did not enter an already good world that simply needed some guidance and improvement. He came into a dark world cursed by sin to a people who were spiritually dead.

Jesus' birth is good news for people who need a Savior. In God the Son's becoming a human, Jesus brought life and light to people who were dead in sin. Jesus came to give life to all who believe. He brought light into darkness and showed us what God is like.

Invite kids to celebrate the birth of Jesus, which brought joy and peace to a desperate and chaotic world. Pray that God would prepare the hearts of all children—from babies to preschoolers to older kids—to hear and believe the truths about Jesus and welcome Him into their lives as Lord and Savior.

The **BIBLE** Story

Jesus Was Born
John 1

John, one of Jesus' disciples, wrote to tell people about who Jesus is. **John wrote that the Word—Jesus—existed in the beginning, before the world even began. The Word** has always **existed with God, and** the Word has always existed **as God.** He was with God in the beginning. **When God spoke at creation, all things were created through His Word.** Not one thing was created apart from Him.

The Word brought life into the world and light for all people. The light shines in the darkness, and the darkness could not hide it.

God sent a man named John the Baptist to be a witness to the light. John was not the light, but he came to **tell people about the light so they might believe.** The true light was coming into the world to give light to everyone.

When Jesus came into the world, people did not recognize Him. His own people did not accept Him. **But this is good news: to everyone who did accept Him, He gave them the right to be part of God's family—to be children of God.**

The Word became a human and lived among us. People saw His glory—the glory of the one and only Son of God. He was full of grace and truth. **John the Baptist told people that even though Jesus came into the world after him, Jesus is greater because He existed before John.** People received blessings from Jesus, grace upon grace. Long ago, God gave people the law through Moses, but now He has given us grace and truth through Jesus Christ.

No one has ever seen God, but Jesus—God's one and only Son—has shown us what God is like.

Christ Connection: The birth of Jesus was good news! Jesus was no ordinary baby. He was God's Son, sent to earth from heaven. Jesus came into the world as a human to bring us life. He brought light into darkness and showed us what God is like.

Bible Storytelling Tips

• **Use space:** Start on one side of the room. When you reach the part of the story where Jesus came to earth, move to the opposite side of the room.

• **Use lighting:** Tell the story in a dim room. When you reach the part of the story about Jesus being a light in the world, use lighting effects to brighten the stage.

INTRODUCE the Story

SESSION TITLE: Jesus Was Born

BIBLE PASSAGE: John 1

STORY POINT: Jesus came to bring us life.

KEY PASSAGE: 2 Peter 1:3

BIG PICTURE QUESTION: How does the Holy Spirit help Christians? The Holy Spirit comforts us, shows us our sin, and guides us as we live for God's glory.

Welcome time

Greet each kid as he or she arrives. Use this time to collect the offering, fill out attendance sheets, and help new kids connect to your group. Prompt kids to discuss how they feel about the dark. Are any of them uncomfortable in a dark room? Discourage any kids from teasing or being rude if some kids are afraid of the dark.

SAY • Being afraid of the dark is a common fear. Even adults are uncomfortable when we cannot see what's around us. Today, we will learn about the light of the world, and how He came into the world to overcome darkness. Not physical darkness, but spiritual darkness. Who do you think the light of the world is?

Activity page (5 minutes)

- "The Word Revealed" activity page, 1 per kid
- pencils or markers

Invite kids to complete the "The Word Revealed" activity page. Instruct kids to cross out the second letter and every other letter after that to reveal a special phrase: *the Word became flesh.*

SAY • What do you think *the Word became flesh* means? Who is the Word? When did He become flesh? We'll talk more about that today.

Session starter (10 minutes)

OPTION 1: Christmas Words

Play a word association game with the kids. Say words associated with Christmas traditions common where you live. Encourage the kids to respond with the first different word they think of. You may record their words on a piece of paper or dry erase board.

Suggested words: Christmas, manger, holly, star, gift, baby, and so forth.

SAY • We have a lot of things we connect in our brains with Christmas. When you think of the holiday, you may think of presents, decorations, or special cookies. The most important part of Christmas is Jesus' coming into the world. We will learn more about Jesus, and why He came to earth as a human.

OPTION 2: Light in the darkness

Provide each kid with a small LED keychain light. Dim the lights in your room and encourage the kids to leave their lights off until you signal them to turn them on one at a time. Do not allow the kids to shine their lights into the faces of others. Direct them to point their lights only straight up.

SAY • It's amazing what a difference a single light can make in a dark room. And each additional light really started to add up. Soon the room didn't feel dark at all! Today, we will learn about the light of the world, and how He came to overcome the darkness of the world. That's what Christmas is all about!

Transition to teach the story

LOW PREP
· piece of paper and pen (optional)
· dry erase board and marker (optional)

· LED keychain lights, 1 per kid

Tip: LED keychain lights can be purchased on many online retail sites. They should cost around 75¢ per light or less if purchased in bulk.

TEACH the Story

SESSION TITLE: Jesus Was Born

BIBLE PASSAGE: John 1

STORY POINT: Jesus came to bring us life.

KEY PASSAGE: 2 Peter 1:3

BIG PICTURE QUESTION: How does the Holy Spirit help Christians? The Holy Spirit comforts us, shows us our sin, and guides us as we live for God's glory.

Countdown

· countdown video

Show the countdown video as you transition to teach the story. Set it to end as the session begins.

Introduce the session (3 minutes)

· leader attire
· Christmas decorations (optional)

Tip: If you prefer not to use themed content or characters, adapt or omit this introduction.

[You may choose to add Christmas decorations over the regular firefighter theme decorations. Leader enters wearing firefighter costume.]

LEADER • Welcome to the station, kids! As you can tell, we decorated for Christmas. I love this time of year. As a firefighter, I spend most of my working time thinking about helping other people because it's my job; but in December, it feels like everyone shifts gears to think about others before themselves, and I really love that.

Firefighters often have the honor of saving someone's life, but there's a kind of salvation that we can never offer. That's the salvation from sins that only Jesus is able to provide. This week, in honor of the Christmas season, let's talk more about Jesus' coming to earth. That's what Christmas is all about, after all!

Big picture question (1 minute)

LEADER • Our big picture question hasn't changed: ***How does the Holy Spirit help Christians? The Holy Spirit comforts us, shows us our sin, and guides us as we live for God's glory.*** The Holy Spirit is the third Person of the Trinity, along with God the Father and God the Son. Each Person is fully God living perfectly united as one God. But only Jesus is also fully human. Jesus came to earth as a human to make the way for us to be saved. When we are saved, the Holy Spirit lives within us to help us honor God through all areas of our life.

Giant timeline (1 minute)

Show the giant timeline. Point to individual Bible stories as you review.

· Giant Timeline

LEADER • Although we've been studying the time after Jesus returned to heaven and sent the Holy Spirit, let's look back at how and why Jesus came to earth. You may expect us to read from Luke 2, and talk about the shepherds who came to see Baby Jesus in the manger. But not this year. Instead, I want to talk about John 1. You may not think of John 1 as a passage that has to do with Christmas, but it tells us more about who Jesus is. Jesus was not just a baby born in Bethlehem. He is God the Son! Let's hear more about it.

· Bibles
· "Jesus Was Born" video
· Big Picture Question Poster
· Bible Story Picture Poster
· Story Point Poster

Tell the Bible story (10 minutes)

Open your Bible to John 1. Use the Bible storytelling tips on the Bible story page to help you tell the story, or show the Bible story video "Jesus Was Born."

LEADER • Bible scholars have spent years studying and thinking about the name John used for Jesus: The Word. In the original language of the Book of John, the Greek word used is *Logos*. *Logos* is the same word from which we get the word *logic*. When John called Jesus the *Word*, he was packing a lot of meaning into a single … well, word!

Jesus is the exact representation of God's character. He is a reflection of God's plans and purpose in the world. He is the logic and reason behind all of creation. When God spoke the world into existence, the Son was there, creating together with God the Father. When John explains that the Word became flesh, he's explaining that the full power, perfection, and glory of God was becoming human. It's incredible to think about, and nearly impossible for us to really understand.

Imagine that you have a tiny, little eye-dropper. Imagine you went to the seashore and squeezed the little rubber bulb and stuck the end into the ocean. Now imagine that when you released the rubber bulb, it sucked in all the water from all the oceans in all the world—and still looked like a regular little eye-dropper. In a way, that can help you think about the miracle it was for God the Son to come to earth as a human baby. Jesus is the light in a dark world. He is the Word who became flesh and dwelt among us. **Jesus came to bring us life**.

Note: You may use this opportunity to use Scripture and the guide provided to explain how to become a Christian. Make sure kids know when and where they can ask questions.

Christ connection

LEADER • The birth of Jesus was good news! Jesus was no ordinary baby. He was God's Son, sent to earth from

46

heaven. Jesus came into the world as a human to bring us life. He brought light into darkness and showed us what God is like.

Questions from kids video (3 minutes)

Show the "Christmas, Session 3" questions from kids video. Prompt kids to think about Jesus' birth. Guide them to discuss how their families celebrate Jesus becoming human.

· "Christmas, Session 3" Questions from Kids video

Missions moment (3 minutes)

Show the pictures from the "Lottie Moon Photos" printable. You may choose to review the facts from the printable used in Unit 28 Session 2 Missions Moment.

LEADER • Lottie Moon lived over 100 years ago. These pictures of her can help us remember her and the work she did for Jesus. Lottie died on Christmas Eve in 1912 after serving in China for 39 years. She knew that **Jesus came to give us life** and she wanted the people of China to have the eternal life that Jesus offers.

· "Lottie Moon Photos" printable
· "Lottie Moon Fact Strips" printable (optional; see Unit 28 Session 2)

Key passage (5 minutes)

Show the key passage poster. Lead the boys and girls to read together 2 Peter 1:3. Then sing "Life and Godliness (2 Peter 1:3)."

LEADER • When Peter wrote these words, he may not have known that we would still be learning them and treasuring them thousands of years later. But they are God's words written through Peter, and they are a wonderful reminder that, in Jesus, we have everything we could ever need and more!

· Key Passage Poster
· "Life and Godliness (2 Peter 1:3)" song

Sing (4 minutes)

LEADER • The same power of God by which Jesus came to earth, lived a perfect life, died the death we deserve, and rose in victory can be ours through the Holy Spirit when we have faith. His power and help are the beginning of the mission for us!

Sing together "This is Where the Mission Begins."

Pray (2 minutes)

Invite kids to pray before dismissing to apply the story.

LEADER • Father, thank You for sending Your Son to live with us as a human. Help us to trust You and dedicate our lives to serving You and glorifying You. Allow us to be a part of Your plans to grow Your kingdom in the world. Use us to spread the gospel to lost people everywhere. Amen.

Dismiss to apply the story

The Gospel: God's Plan for Me

Ask kids if they have ever heard the word *gospel*. Clarify that the word *gospel* means "good news." It is the message about Christ, the kingdom of God, and salvation. Use the following guide to share the gospel with kids.

God rules. Explain to kids that the Bible tells us God created everything, and He is in charge of everything. Invite a volunteer to read Genesis 1:1 from the Bible. Read Revelation 4:11 or Colossians 1:16-17 aloud and explain what these verses mean.

We sinned. Tell kids that since the time of Adam and Eve, everyone has chosen to disobey God. (Romans 3:23) The Bible calls this sin. Because God is holy, God cannot be around sin. Sin separates us from God and deserves God's punishment of death. (Romans 6:23)

God provided. Choose a child to read John 3:16 aloud. Say that God sent His Son, Jesus, the perfect solution to our sin problem, to rescue us from the punishment we deserve. It's something we, as sinners, could never earn on our own. Jesus alone saves us. Read and explain Ephesians 2:8-9.

Jesus gives. Share with kids that Jesus lived a perfect life, died on the cross for our sins, and rose again. Because Jesus gave up His life for us, we can be welcomed into God's family for eternity. This is the best gift ever! Read Romans 5:8; 2 Corinthians 5:21; or 1 Peter 3:18.

We respond. Tell kids that they can respond to Jesus. Read Romans 10:9-10,13. Review these aspects of our response: Believe in your heart that Jesus alone saves you through what He's already done on the cross. Repent, turning from self and sin to Jesus. Tell God and others that your faith is in Jesus.

Offer to talk with any child who is interested in responding to Jesus. Provide *I'm a Christian Now!* for new Christians to take home and complete with their families.

APPLY the Story

SESSION TITLE: Jesus Was Born
BIBLE PASSAGE: John 1
STORY POINT: Jesus came to bring us life.
KEY PASSAGE: 2 Peter 1:3
BIG PICTURE QUESTION: How does the Holy Spirit help Christians? The Holy Spirit comforts us, shows us our sin, and guides us as we live for God's glory.

Key passage activity (5 minutes)

· Key Passage Poster

Challenge volunteers to say the verse from memory. Thank each kid's effort and encourage all the kids to continue working to memorize the key passage. Then, set the key passage to the tune of a Christmas song your group is familiar with and sing it together multiple times.

SAY • Peter wrote these words to believers who were facing persecution. They were being treated badly, hurt, and even killed because of their faith in Jesus. Peter wanted them to know that the Holy Spirit was with them, and He gave them all the power they needed to live for God's glory. *How does the Holy Spirit help Christians? The Holy Spirit comforts us, shows us our sin, and guides us as we live for God's glory.*

Discussion & Bible skills (10 minutes)

· Bibles, 1 per kid
· Story Point Poster
· Small Group Timeline and Map Set (005802970, optional)

Distribute a Bible to each kid. Help them find John 1. Remind the kids that John is in the Gospels division of the New Testament. Ask them which book comes right before John and which comes right after. (*Luke, Acts*) Explain that even though John 1 doesn't specifically talk about Jesus' birth in Bethlehem, it's about His coming to earth as Savior.

Ask the following questions. Lead the group to discuss:

1. Who existed in the beginning with God? (*The Word, John 1:1*)
2. Who came to tell about the light coming into the world? (*John the Baptist, John 1:6-9*)
3. What did Jesus show us when He became human? (*What God is like and His love for us, John 1:14-18*)
4. How do we receive "grace and truth" through Jesus? *Guide kids to see that everyone who repents and believes the gospel is saved. We receive the truth of the gospel as a gift from God and His grace saves us from our sin. Apart from Jesus, no one can receive grace and truth.*
5. What does it mean for Jesus to be the light of the world? *Discuss the fact that, although we think of light and darkness as opposites, darkness is really the lack of light. Light and darkness don't clash and cancel one another out, light always defeats darkness and pushes it back. Jesus' work on the cross defeated sin and death—spiritual darkness—overcoming it completely.*
6. Why is it important to understand who Jesus is beyond just a baby born two thousand years ago? *Help kids think through the importance of Jesus' identity as God the Son. Remind them that His full humanity combined with His full diety made Him the only One who could provide the perfect sacrifice. Jesus' birth is important because it marked the moment God came to earth to save us from sin.*

SAY • **Jesus came to bring us life.** Jesus' life did not just teach us about God, it set the stage for Him to give us eternal life through His death and resurrection.

Option: Retell or review the Bible story using the bolded text of the Bible story script.

LOW PREP

· "Lottie Moon Photos" printable
· scissors
· tape
· ribbon

Tip: Use this activity option to reinforce the missions moment found in Teach the Story.

Activity choice (10 minutes)

OPTION 1: Lottie Moon

Distribute copies of the "Lottie Moon Photos" printable. Invite kids to cut out one of the photos and tape a loop of ribbon to the back. Allow the kids to take the ornaments to hang somewhere in their home.

SAY • At Christmastime, we celebrate that **Jesus came to bring us life**. Lottie Moon wanted everyone to know that truth, and she dedicated her life to teaching people in China about Jesus. You can take these ornaments home to hang somewhere. When you see your ornament, you can be encouraged to live on mission for Jesus!

· heavyweight paper
· markers
· glitter pens, stickers, and other craft supplies

OPTION 2: Christmas cards

Provide the kids with heavyweight paper, markers, glitter pens, Christmas stickers, and other craft supplies. Encourage the kids to make Christmas cards for their friends or neighbors. Help them write the story point in the card, or another message about Jesus or the gospel.

SAY • Christmastime is a great reason to give cards to people. We can use cards like these to help us share the gospel and show love to those around us. **Jesus came to bring us life**, and the Holy Spirit helps us tell others about the wonderful life Jesus brought!

Reflection and prayer (5 minutes)

· pencils and crayons
· paper
· Bible Story Coloring Page, 1 per kid

Distribute a sheet of paper to each child. Ask the kids to write about or draw a picture to answer the following questions:

• What does this story teach me about God or about the gospel?

- What does this story teach me about myself?
- Whom can I tell about this story?

Make sure to send the sheets home with kids alongside the activity page so that parents can see what their kids have been learning.

If time remains, take prayer requests or allow kids to complete the Bible story coloring page provided with this session. Pray for your group.

Tip: Give parents this week's Big Picture Cards for Families to allow families to interact with the biblical content at home.

Unit 28 · Session 3
Faithful in Hard Times

BIBLE PASSAGE:
1 Peter 1–2

STORY POINT:
Peter encouraged believers who faced persecution.

KEY PASSAGE:
2 Peter 1:3

BIG PICTURE QUESTION:
How does the Holy Spirit help Christians? The Holy Spirit comforts us, shows us our sin, and guides us as we live for God's glory.

INTRODUCE THE STORY (10–15 MINUTES) **PAGE 58**		**TEACH THE STORY** (25–30 MINUTES) **PAGE 60**		**APPLY THE STORY** (25–30 MINUTES) **PAGE 66**
	→		→	

Leaders, grow on the go! Listen to session-by-session training every week on Ministry Grid, Apple Podcasts, Spotify, or LifeWay's Digital Pass:
ministrygrid.com/gospelproject | gospelproject.com/podcasts

LEADER Bible Study

Peter's story of faith began when Jesus said, "Follow Me." (Matt. 4:18) Peter and his brother Andrew—two fishermen from Galilee—left their nets and followed Jesus. As one of Jesus' twelve disciples, Peter witnessed firsthand Jesus' miracles and teachings.

Peter believed that Jesus is the Messiah (Matt. 16:16), and he was understandably upset when Jesus predicted that Peter would deny Him (Matt. 26:34-35). Peter fell asleep as Jesus prayed in the garden, and he drew his sword to defend Jesus when He was arrested. (Matt. 26:40; John 18:10) Peter denied Jesus three times, but after the resurrection Jesus appeared to Peter and the other disciples. Then Jesus restored Peter to ministry at the sea of Galilee. (John 21:15-19)

The first 12 chapters in the Book of Acts record the Holy Spirit's work through Peter after Pentecost. God revealed to Peter that the gospel is for everyone—Jews and Gentiles. Peter was arrested and imprisoned for sharing the gospel, but an angel of the Lord rescued him. (Acts 12:1-8)

Peter wrote his first letter sometime between AD 62 and 64 to believers who had experienced persecution and suffering. He encouraged them and reminded them how to live holy lives as followers of Christ, looking forward to an eternal reward in their true home—heaven.

Peter's letter was written nearly two thousand years ago to believers who were not far removed from Jesus' life on earth. We still wait eagerly for Jesus' return, but God calls us to faithfulness in hard times—using our time on earth to better know and love Him, and to tell others about Him. As believers, we are all called to live a life of love and to glorify God by what we do and say, even in the midst of trials and troubles.

The BIBLE Story

Faithful in Hard Times
1 Peter 1–2

In the early church, **Jesus' followers faced persecution.** The disciples told others about Jesus, but some people did not like what they were saying. Those people mistreated the believers because of their faith, and many believers were forced to leave their homes and go to different cities.

Peter, one of Jesus' disciples, **wrote a letter to encourage them.** Peter was a leader in the church, and he wanted to help these believers be faithful in hard times.

Peter said, **"Praise God! He is merciful and has given us new life. We have hope because of Jesus, whom God raised from the dead."** Peter reminded believers that **because we are children of God, we have blessings in heaven that cannot be taken away or destroyed.** We rejoice in this promise, even though we face suffering in this life. **When hard times happen, God is honored as we trust Him by faith.**

Peter also wrote, "Hope in Jesus and be holy. God is your Father; live in a way that shows Him respect." **Peter reminded the believers that before they trusted in Jesus, they lived however they wanted. Jesus gave His life to save them so they could have** a better life—**true life through His Word.**

Peter said, "This world is not your home. Do not live like people around you who do wrong things. Instead, do what is good. Live as servants of God. Show love and respect to everyone. Others will see your good works and give glory to God."

Jesus gave us an example to follow. He suffered for us, dying for our sins so that we could live for what is right. Before, we were like lost sheep. Now Jesus is our Shepherd.

Christ Connection: The Bible says Christians will suffer for following Jesus. Peter encouraged believers who faced persecution for their faith. Through suffering, God can make us more like His Son. Jesus gives us hope and true life so we can live joyfully for Him, even in hard times.

• **Doodle it:** Sketch simple drawings and shapes to represent the parts of the story you are speaking about.

The Holy Spirit Empowers

INTRODUCE the Story

SESSION TITLE: Faithful in Hard Times

BIBLE PASSAGE: 1 Peter 1–2

STORY POINT: Peter encouraged believers who faced persecution.

KEY PASSAGE: 2 Peter 1:3

BIG PICTURE QUESTION: How does the Holy Spirit help Christians? The Holy Spirit comforts us, shows us our sin, and guides us as we live for God's glory.

Welcome time

Greet each kid as he or she arrives. Use this time to collect the offering, fill out attendance sheets, and help new kids connect to your group. Prompt kids to discuss a time they felt sad, scared, or alone. Be alert and sensitive if any kids discloses abuse or neglect. Always follow reporting procedures according to the laws where you live and your ministry's policies.

SAY • We all face situations where we feel sad, scared, or alone. Thankfully, God sent the Holy Spirit to help us when we have faith in Jesus. That means we are never truly alone! Today we will learn about a time Peter wrote a letter to encourage Christians who felt sad, scared, and alone.

Activity page (5 minutes)

- "Hidden in Plain Sight" activity page, 1 per kid
- pencils or markers

Invite kids to complete the "Hidden in Plain Sight" activity page. Use the key provided to find the shapes hidden in the Bible story picture.

SAY • Believers facing persecution might be tempted to try and blend in so people don't know they have faith in Jesus. Do you think that's a wise choice?

Session starter (10 minutes)

OPTION 1: Easy or Hard?

Provide different scenarios to the kids. Ask them to vote on whether they think the situation would be easy or hard. Allow a few kids to explain why they voted the way they voted. Use the suggested scenarios or come up with your own. Play as time allows.

Suggestions:

- Your mom told you not to eat more cookies, but she's busy and wouldn't see you sneak one.
- Your friend's pet died, and you don't know how to comfort her.
- Some kids are picking on a new student at your school. If you stick up for him, they might pick on you as well.

SAY • We all face hard situations sometimes. Doing the right thing can often feel like a huge challenge. Who do you think helps us choose the right things?

OPTION 2: Steadfast and strong

Select a kid to be the watchman. He will stand in the center of the room. The rest of the kids will scatter around the room. Kids must sneak toward the watchman to gently touch his shoulder. However, kids may only move when the watchman isn't looking at them. If the watchman catches a kid moving, he or she must take five large steps away from the watchman.

SAY • It can be hard to stand firm like a statue. It can also be hard to "stand firm" in your faith when facing hard times. Let's learn more about that today!

Transition to teach the story

TEACH the Story

SESSION TITLE: Faithful in Hard Times
BIBLE PASSAGE: 1 Peter 1–2
STORY POINT: Peter encouraged believers who faced persecution.
KEY PASSAGE: 2 Peter 1:3
BIG PICTURE QUESTION: How does the Holy Spirit help Christians? The Holy Spirit comforts us, shows us our sin, and guides us as we live for God's glory.

Countdown

· countdown video

Show the countdown video as you transition to teach the story. Set it to end as the session begins.

Introduce the session (3 minutes)

· leader attire

[Leader enters wearing firefighter costume.]

Tip: If you prefer not to use themed content or characters, adapt or omit this introduction.

LEADER • Hey everyone. I'm glad to see you today. We recently had a new group of potential firefighter recruits go through the preliminary training. We started with 50, but that number has dropped to just 13. Being a firefighter is hard work, so the training program to onboard new firefighters has to be tough. If you can't make it through the training, you definitely can't join the station.

When your life and the lives of your co-workers all depend on each member being ready for the challenges ahead, it's vital that no one has cut corners or taken the easy way out. That means that when we say you have to climb a ladder in less than two minutes while carrying nearly 100 pounds of firefighter gear, we mean it has to be done in two minutes or less. Only those who can persevere in

Younger Kids Leader Guide
Unit 28 • Session 3

trials can make the team. That's why only 13 of the 50 recruits are left. The rest gave up or couldn't perform the tasks.

In our Bible story, we will learn about a time Peter encouraged believers who faced hard times. He told them not to give up and not to lose hope, but to keep trusting God even in sad or scary circumstances.

Big picture question (1 minute)

LEADER • The Holy Spirit inspired Peter to write his letters to believers, and those letters contained comforting words and encouragement to Christians who faced persecution for their faith. That's just one way the Holy Spirit helps us. *How does the Holy Spirit help Christians? The Holy Spirit comforts us, shows us our sin, and guides us as we live for God's glory.* God wants us to live our lives in obedience to Him, and with the Holy Spirit's help, we really can do that!

Giant timeline (1 minute)

Show the giant timeline. Point to individual Bible stories as you review.   · Giant Timeline

LEADER • Soon after Jesus returned to heaven, **God kept His promise to send the Holy Spirit**. After that, the apostles began to do mighty works by His power. **The Holy Spirit gave Peter power to heal a man.** This week, we will learn about a time the Holy Spirit inspired Peter to write a letter to encourage believers who faced *persecution*—hateful treatment because of their faith in Jesus. Our story is called "Faithful in Hard Times."

Tell the Bible story (10 minutes)

Open your Bible to 1 Peter 1–2. Use the Bible storytelling tips on the Bible story page to help you tell the story, or show the Bible story video "Faithful in Hard Times."

LEADER • While Jesus was on earth, one of the things He taught was that all Christians would face persecution. As always, Jesus' words were true. After Jesus went back to heaven, believers faced lots of persecution from those who did not believe Jesus was God's Son.

Peter knew that the benefits of loving and following Jesus were worth any kind of persecution we might face, so his letter aimed to remind believers what was true. He wanted them to know that God's love for them was real. God had adopted them into His family, and no one could take that away.

The suffering we face in life is an opportunity to show the world what Jesus is like. When we face suffering with love, patience, and faithfulness, it provides a picture of the love, patience, and faithfulness God has shown to us.

Every single Christian was born in sin, an enemy of God. It is only through God's love and grace that anyone can be saved. For those of us who are saved, all the hard times we face in life are temporary. The eternal life we get through faith will outlast all the sadness of our broken world. Peter reminded Christians that our home isn't the world as it is now—broken by sin. Our home is the perfectly restored world that Jesus will bring when He returns.

Christ connection

LEADER • The Bible says Christians will suffer for following

- Bibles
- "Faithful in Hard Times" video
- Big Picture Question Poster
- Bible Story Picture Poster
- Story Point Poster

Note: You may use this opportunity to use Scripture and the guide provided to explain how to become a Christian. Make sure kids know when and where they can ask questions.

Jesus. **Peter encouraged believers who faced persecution** for their faith. Through suffering, God can make us more like His Son. Jesus gives us hope and true life so we can live joyfully for Him, even in hard times.

Questions from kids video (3 minutes)

Show the "Unit 28, Session 3" questions from kids video. Prompt kids to think about who is in control of all things. Guide them to discuss how hard times can bring us closer to God.

· "Unit 28, Session 3" Questions from Kids video

Missions moment (3 minutes)

Print a copy of the "Lottie's Faithfulness" printable. Invite a strong reader to read the story aloud.

· "Lottie's Faithfuness" printable

LEADER • Lottie was faithful, even when she faced persecution for following Jesus. Through her faithfulness, she encouraged others to stand strong for Jesus. This week, let's remember to pray for missionaries, especially [*names of missionaries your church supports*]. Ask God to give them boldness to share the gospel with everyone they meet.

Key passage (5 minutes)

Show the key passage poster. Lead the boys and girls to read together 2 Peter 1:3. Then sing "Life and Godliness (2 Peter 1:3)."

· Key Passage Poster
· "Life and Godliness (2 Peter 1:3)" song

LEADER • Through the Holy Spirit, we have everything we need to live for God. God knows everything. He created us and knows what is best for us. When we live for His glory, we are also living for our own good! This key passage helps us remember that truth.

Sing (4 minutes)

· "This is Where the Mission Begins" song

LEADER • Jesus gave us an important mission when He went back to heaven. Then, Jesus sent us the Holy Spirit to help us obey Jesus' commands. The mission begins for all believers as soon as we believe and receive the Holy Spirit.

Sing together "This is Where the Mission Begins."

Pray (2 minutes)

Invite kids to pray before dismissing to apply the story.

LEADER • Lord, thank You for giving us Your Son. Thank You for sending the Holy Spirit to live with us and help us glorify You with our whole lives. Give us courage to face hard times and remain faithful to You no matter what. We love You. Amen.

Dismiss to apply the story

The Gospel: God's Plan for Me

Ask kids if they have ever heard the word *gospel*. Clarify that the word *gospel* means "good news." It is the message about Christ, the kingdom of God, and salvation. Use the following guide to share the gospel with kids.

God rules. Explain to kids that the Bible tells us God created everything, and He is in charge of everything. Invite a volunteer to read Genesis 1:1 from the Bible. Read Revelation 4:11 or Colossians 1:16-17 aloud and explain what these verses mean.

We sinned. Tell kids that since the time of Adam and Eve, everyone has chosen to disobey God. (Romans 3:23) The Bible calls this sin. Because God is holy, God cannot be around sin. Sin separates us from God and deserves God's punishment of death. (Romans 6:23)

God provided. Choose a child to read John 3:16 aloud. Say that God sent His Son, Jesus, the perfect solution to our sin problem, to rescue us from the punishment we deserve. It's something we, as sinners, could never earn on our own. Jesus alone saves us. Read and explain Ephesians 2:8-9.

Jesus gives. Share with kids that Jesus lived a perfect life, died on the cross for our sins, and rose again. Because Jesus gave up His life for us, we can be welcomed into God's family for eternity. This is the best gift ever! Read Romans 5:8; 2 Corinthians 5:21; or 1 Peter 3:18.

We respond. Tell kids that they can respond to Jesus. Read Romans 10:9-10,13. Review these aspects of our response: Believe in your heart that Jesus alone saves you through what He's already done on the cross. Repent, turning from self and sin to Jesus. Tell God and others that your faith is in Jesus.

Offer to talk with any child who is interested in responding to Jesus. Provide *I'm a Christian Now!* for new Christians to take home and complete with their families.

APPLY the Story

SESSION TITLE: Faithful in Hard Times

BIBLE PASSAGE: 1 Peter 1–2

STORY POINT: Peter encouraged believers who faced persecution.

KEY PASSAGE: 2 Peter 1:3

BIG PICTURE QUESTION: How does the Holy Spirit help Christians? The Holy Spirit comforts us, shows us our sin, and guides us as we live for God's glory.

Key passage activity (5 minutes)

· Key Passage Poster
· index cards
· pen

Write each word of the key passage on a separate index card Challenge the kids to say the key passage from memory, and use the index cards to either reveal as the kids say the key passage, or use as prompts to help them remember what comes next.

SAY • Our key passage comes from words Peter wrote in the second letter of his in the Bible. Peter wrote to churches who faced lots of persecution. They were being mistreated, hurt, and even killed for their faith. Peter's words came directly from God and reminded people that their power to live in hard times came from the Holy Spirit. He provides everything a believer needs!

Discussion & Bible skills (10 minutes)

· Bibles, 1 per kid
· Story Point Poster
· Small Group Timeline and Map Set
  (005802970, optional)

Distribute a Bible to each kid. Help them find 1 Peter 1. Explain that 1 Peter is part of the General Letters division of the New Testament. The apostle Peter wrote this letter around 30 years after Jesus' ascension. It's not known for sure, but it's likely Peter wrote from Rome. (*B1* on the New Testament Mediterranean Map)

Ask the following questions. Lead the group to discuss:

Option: Retell or review the Bible story using the bolded text of the Bible story script.

1. What did Peter say we are born into when we have faith in Jesus? (*blessings in heaven, a perfect inheritance; 1 Peter 1:4*)

2. What reason did Peter give for us to be faithful in hard times? (*it honors God, 1 Peter 2:12*)

3. Why did Peter say Jesus bore our sins? (*So that we could live for righteousness; 1 Peter 2:24*)

4. What does it mean to live for righteousness? *Guide kids to discuss what righteousness is. Talk through what the Bible says about righteousness. Remind them that we only have righteousness through faith in Jesus' righteousness. Help them see that we are saved from sin, so we can choose obedience.*

5. What is our inheritance from God? *Explain to kids what an inheritance is, and talk about what we receive from God as a result of being adopted into His family. Remind them that we gain eternal life with God, joy, peace, wisdom, mercy and grace. Spend time explaining each of those concepts if kids do not understand them.*

6. Why does God allow us to face hard times? *Discuss the benefits of facing hard times, such as growing in patience, learning to trust God more, and showing His power and love to the world by responding graciously to those who are cruel to us. Remind kids that God can turn all things to good, and that even when we don't see the good He is working out.*

SAY • **Peter encouraged believers who faced persecution.** Jesus promised us that we would go through struggles as a result of our faith. We can trust Jesus no matter what, and know that all our struggles will be worth it because of our eternal life with God.

Activity choice (10 minutes)

OPTION 1: Secret Bibles

Play a simple game of "Pass the Bible." Ask for one volunteer to be a guard who is trying to catch people giving Bibles. The volunteer should stand with his or her back to the group. Ask the other kids to sit next to each other and quietly pass the Bible to one another. The "guard" can turn at any time and try to guess who has the Bible or "catch" the person with the Bible. If the guard knows who has the Bible, that person goes to "jail" (sits against a wall). Continue to play for several rounds.

SAY • In many places around the world, it is illegal to be a Christian. Sometime you can be punished just for owning a Bible. In those places, Christians must be very careful when they use their Bibles and who they give Bibles to. Persecution happened to Lottie Moon, and it still happens today. We can pray that God will help believers remain faithful in hard times.

OPTION 2: Encouraging words

Invite the kids to sit in a circle. Select a kid to start the game by saying one encouraging thing to the kid on her left. Then it will be his turn to say something encouraging to the kid on his left, and so forth around the circle. You may provide each kid with an index card and a pen or pencil so they can write down the kind things said about them by others. Be prepared to help kids who seem shy or stuck.

SAY • God created people to live together in community. That's one of the reasons it feels so nice to be told encouraging things.

When Christians in Peter's day were facing terrible

LOW PREP

· Bible

Tip: Use this activity option to reinforce the missions moment found in Teach the Story.

· index cards (optional)
· pens or pencils (optional)

persecution, Peter wrote them a letter to remind them of the most encouraging thing of all: God loves us and sent Jesus to save us from our sin. Whenever we feel sad, lonely, or afraid, we need to remember Jesus' love and the power of the Holy Spirit too.

Reflection and prayer (5 minutes)

Distribute a sheet of paper to each child. Ask the kids to write about or draw a picture to answer the following questions:

- What does this story teach me about God or about the gospel?
- What does this story teach me about myself?
- Whom can I tell about this story?

Make sure to send the sheets home with kids alongside the activity page so that parents can see what their kids have been learning.

If time remains, take prayer requests or allow kids to complete the Bible story coloring page provided with this session. Pray for your group.

- pencils and crayons
- paper
- Bible Story Coloring Page, 1 per kid

Tip: Give parents this week's Big Picture Cards for Families to allow families to interact with the biblical content at home.

Unit 28 · Session 4
Living Like Jesus

BIBLE PASSAGE:
2 Peter 1

STORY POINT:
Peter instructed believers
to live like Jesus.

KEY PASSAGE:
2 Peter 1:3

BIG PICTURE QUESTION:
How does the Holy Spirit help
Christians? The Holy Spirit comforts us,
shows us our sin, and guides us as we live
for God's glory.

INTRODUCE THE STORY
(10–15 MINUTES)
PAGE 74

→

TEACH THE STORY
(25–30 MINUTES)
PAGE 76

→

APPLY THE STORY
(25–30 MINUTES)
PAGE 82

Leaders, grow on the go! Listen to session-by-session training every week on
Ministry Grid, Apple Podcasts, Spotify, or LifeWay's Digital Pass:
ministrygrid.com/gospelproject | gospelproject.com/podcasts

LEADER Bible Study

Like his first letter, Peter's second letter was written to believers in the early church who had experienced persecution and suffering. At this time, Peter was in a Roman prison. He was aware that his death was imminent. (See 2 Pet. 1:13-15.) Besides the outside threats to their faith, these believers were also confronted with false teachers within the church who tried to lead them away from the true gospel.

Peter warned against false teachers. In the opening chapter of his letter, Peter's exhortation to live like Jesus gives believers a measure for making sure they are following the truth. The best defense against false teachers is a dedication to a knowledge of the truth. As you prepare to teach from 2 Peter 1, consider these two questions: How do we live like Jesus? Why do we live like Jesus?

First, God's people live like Jesus through the power of Jesus (2 Pet. 1:3-4) and through personal application (2 Pet. 1:5-7). Not only is the Christian life marked by faith in Christ, it is characterized by goodness, knowledge, self-control, endurance, godliness, brotherly affection, and love. These come from knowing Jesus, who calls us to Himself.

Second, God's people live like Jesus to confirm their calling. (2 Pet. 1:8-11) If we claim to have faith but do not live like Jesus, we have forgotten what Jesus has done for us. Because God has credited to us Jesus' righteousness, we strive to live in loving obedience to Him to show those around us that Jesus has truly changed our lives.

Soon after writing this letter, Peter was killed in Rome as Jesus had predicted. (John 21:18-19) Help kids grasp that Jesus lived a perfect life and died the death we deserve for our sin. When we trust in Jesus, God forgives our sins and changes our hearts. Jesus calls and empowers His followers to live like Him.

Living Like Jesus

2 Peter 1

Peter was one of Jesus' disciples who became a leader in the early church. He **wrote two letters in the Bible to help believers who were facing hard times.** When **Peter wrote his second letter,** he was **in a Roman prison. He had been arrested because he was a follower of Jesus.**

Peter wrote, **"We have everything we need because we know Jesus.** When we trust in His righteousness, **He gives us power to live for Him.** He is good, and He promises us good things. So this is how we should seek to live. **Along with faith, seek these things: goodness, knowledge, self-control, patience, brotherly affection, and love."** When we have these qualities, Jesus will be glorified in our lives. **When we remember the good promises God has for us, we can rely on His power to resist temptation.**

Peter wanted the believers to **remember** what Jesus had done for them. **Jesus did the greatest work by dying on the cross.** He has taken away our sins! **Because of Jesus, God invites us into His kingdom and gives us eternal life.** Peter wrote, **"God has chosen you and given you His power, so do everything you can to live like Jesus."**

Peter knew he was going to die soon, so he also wrote, "You already know what I'm telling you. I want to keep reminding you as long as I am living so that you will remember even after I'm gone. We did not tell you made-up stories. We told you what we saw and heard."

Christ Connection: Jesus lived a perfect life and died the death we deserve for our sin. When we trust in Jesus, God forgives our sins and changes our hearts. Jesus calls and empowers His followers to live like Him.

Bible Storytelling Tips

- **Alter your voice:** Use a slight variation in your voice to distinguish the quotes from the rest of the story.
- **Dress the part:** Wear Bible times clothing and pretend you are a person from Peter's day explaining what he wrote to your church

INTRODUCE the Story

SESSION TITLE: Living Like Jesus

BIBLE PASSAGE: 2 Peter 1

STORY POINT: Peter instructed believers to live like Jesus.

KEY PASSAGE: 2 Peter 1:3

BIG PICTURE QUESTION: How does the Holy Spirit help Christians? The Holy Spirit comforts us, shows us our sin, and guides us as we live for God's glory.

Welcome time

Greet each kid as he or she arrives. Use this time to collect the offering, fill out attendance sheets, and help new kids connect to your group. Prompt kids to discuss who they consider their heroes and role models. Who do they want to be like when they grow up?

SAY • It's good to have kind, responsible, brave people to look up to, but there's only one person who is the perfect example of how to live—Jesus! Jesus is God's Son, and the only perfect human to ever live. When we put our faith in Him and obey His commands, we live as God wants us to. Can you think of some ways Jesus lived that we should try to copy?

Activity page (5 minutes)

· "Everything You Need" activity page, 1 per kid
· pencils or markers

Invite kids to complete the "Everything You Need" activity page. Ask kids to draw or list everything they can think of that they would need to get through a normal weekday.

SAY • We need a lot of things to get through a typical school day. Today we will talk about the way God gives us everything we need to live like Jesus. Through whom does God give us what we need?

Session starter (10 minutes)

OPTION 1: Desert island

Provide each kid with three index cards. Ask kids to write or draw three things—one per index card—they would take with them if they knew they were going to be stranded on a desert island. After giving them a few minutes to think and write, ask them to compare their answers with one another. Allow them to swap cards if they would like to.

SAY • Trying to plan what you might take with you to a desert island is hard. Should you take only things you need, like food and clothing? Or should you take something for entertainment too? Today we are going to learn what Peter said believers need to live like Jesus. What do you think we need?

OPTION 2: Copycat pictures

Provide each kid with two sheets of paper. Instruct each kid to draw a picture on one of the sheets. After about five minutes, instruct the kids to swap pictures with one another and use the rest of the time trying to copy the swapped picture onto their second sheet of paper. Encourage kids not to trace, but to try re-drawing the picture on their own.

SAY • It's not easy to perfectly copy someone else's work. Usually, it's better to come up with your own art than try to copy someone else's. Today, we will learn about a time when being a copycat is actually good! Who do you think we should copy?

Transition to teach the story

LOW PREP

· index cards
· pens or pencils
· crayons or markers (optional)

· paper
· crayons, markers, or colored pencils

TEACH the Story

SESSION TITLE: Living Like Jesus

BIBLE PASSAGE: 2 Peter 1

STORY POINT: Peter instructed believers to live like Jesus.

KEY PASSAGE: 2 Peter 1:3

BIG PICTURE QUESTION: How does the Holy Spirit help Christians? The Holy Spirit comforts us, shows us our sin, and guides us as we live for God's glory.

Countdown

· countdown video

Show the countdown video as you transition to teach the story. Set it to end as the session begins.

Introduce the session (3 minutes)

· leader attire

[Leader enters wearing firefighter costume.]

Tip: If you prefer not to use themed content or characters, adapt or omit this introduction.

LEADER • Hey everyone. Good to see each of you here today. Some of you have been coming week after week, but for those of you who are new, I'm firefighter [*your name*]. I have a question for you all. Do you trust firefighters? [*Allow responses*]. It's important that firefighters be trustworthy because in an emergency your lives might be in our hands.

If firefighters lived in a way that made us seem untrustworthy, as though we don't have your best interest in mind, it's possible that when you need to listen to us for your own good, you would ignore our warning. That could have disastrous results. That's why firefighters follow a special set of rules called the Firefighter's Code of Ethics.

In a way, this reminds me of our Bible story. When a person has faith in Jesus, she cannot go on living

Younger Kids Leader Guide
Unit 28 • Session 4

however she pleases. It's important that all of us who say we love Jesus live in a way that proves what we say is true. Peter wrote a letter to believers that talked about this truth.

Big picture question (1 minute)

LEADER • Let's review our big picture question and answer. *How does the Holy Spirit help Christians? The Holy Spirit comforts us, shows us our sin, and guides us as we live for God's glory.* This means that when we face hard times, the Holy Spirit will help us feel better and persevere. When we are tempted to or choose to disobey God, the Holy Spirit will remind us the way God wants us to live. When we aren't sure what to do, the Holy Spirit gives us wisdom to understand God's Word and obey it to show God's glory in the world.

Giant timeline (1 minute)

Show the giant timeline. Point to individual Bible stories as you review.

· Giant Timeline

LEADER • It wasn't long after **God kept His promise to send the Holy Spirit** that the apostles began doing mighty works through His power. **The Holy Spirit gave Peter power to heal a man**. He also inspired Peter to write letters to help believers. Last week we learned about a letter Peter wrote in which **Peter encouraged believers who faced persecution**. This week we will learn about a second letter Peter wrote that was inspired by the Holy Spirit. Our story today is called "Living Like Jesus."

Tell the Bible story (10 minutes)

- Bibles
- "Living Like Jesus" video
- Big Picture Question Poster
- Bible Story Picture Poster
- Story Point Poster

Open your Bible to 2 Peter 1. Use the Bible storytelling tips on the Bible story page to help you tell the story, or show the Bible story video "Living Like Jesus."

LEADER • Peter wrote his second letter from a Roman prison. He knew about persecution! And what's more, Jesus knew about persecution. Jesus' death and resurrection made the way for us to live with God forever. It also made the way for us to live for God forever. The Holy Spirit lives with believers and helps us to glorify God in our thoughts, words, and actions. In fact, that's been our big picture question and answer for these last few sessions.

How does the Holy Spirit help Christians? The Holy Spirit comforts us, shows us our sin, and guides us as we live for God's glory. Peter wanted believers to know that living for God is what we are designed to do. Peter instructed believers to live like Jesus. That means we are to show to others the same love, mercy, forgiveness, and compassion that Jesus showed to us. Each day, the Holy Spirit will work through us to make us more like Jesus.

Christ connection

Note: You may use this opportunity to use Scripture and the guide provided to explain how to become a Christian. Make sure kids know when and where they can ask questions.

LEADER • Jesus lived a perfect life and died the death we deserve for our sin. When we trust in Jesus, God forgives our sins and changes our hearts. Jesus calls and empowers His followers to live like Him. We cannot earn salvation by trying to live like Jesus, but when we have salvation through faith in Jesus, the Holy Spirit allows us to live in ways that honor God.

Younger Kids Leader Guide
Unit 28 • Session 4

Questions from kids video (3 minutes)

Show the "Unit 28, Session 4" questions from kids video. Prompt kids to think about how Jesus behaved even when facing temptations, trials, or persecution. Guide them to discuss ways they are becoming like Jesus, and ways they still need to grow in godliness.

- "Unit 28, Session 4" Questions from Kids video

Missions moment (3 minutes)

Play the "Thank You for Giving" missions video.

LEADER • When churches give to missions, they help provide for missionaries to go all over the world and share the gospel. Like Peter, the missionaries encourage believers to live a godly life in an ungodly world. Missionaries appreciate the generosity of believers who help them obey God's command to go and make disciples.

- "Thank You for Giving" missions video

Key passage (5 minutes)

Show the key passage poster. Lead the boys and girls to read together 2 Peter 1:3. Then sing "Life and Godliness (2 Peter 1:3)."

LEADER • This key passage comes from Peter's second letter. Through the Holy Spirit, we have everything we need to live godly lives that point others to Jesus.

- Key Passage Poster
- "Life and Godliness (2 Peter 1:3)" song

Sing (4 minutes)

LEADER • With the Holy Spirit's help, we can live on mission. For each of us, the mission of spreading the gospel begins and ends with the power of God in our lives to make us more like Christ.

Sing together "This is Where the Mission Begins."

- "This is Where the Mission Begins" song

The Holy Spirit Empowers

79

Pray (2 minutes)

Invite kids to pray before dismissing to apply the story.

LEADER • Father, thank You for making us more like Jesus each day. Help us to see the ways You are working in our lives. Help us to be honest about the ways we still need to grow. Give us humble hearts that want to obey You. Give us boldness to live on mission. Amen.

Dismiss to apply the story

The Gospel: God's Plan for Me

Ask kids if they have ever heard the word *gospel*. Clarify that the word *gospel* means "good news." It is the message about Christ, the kingdom of God, and salvation. Use the following guide to share the gospel with kids.

God rules. Explain to kids that the Bible tells us God created everything, and He is in charge of everything. Invite a volunteer to read Genesis 1:1 from the Bible. Read Revelation 4:11 or Colossians 1:16-17 aloud and explain what these verses mean.

We sinned. Tell kids that since the time of Adam and Eve, everyone has chosen to disobey God. (Romans 3:23) The Bible calls this sin. Because God is holy, God cannot be around sin. Sin separates us from God and deserves God's punishment of death. (Romans 6:23)

God provided. Choose a child to read John 3:16 aloud. Say that God sent His Son, Jesus, the perfect solution to our sin problem, to rescue us from the punishment we deserve. It's something we, as sinners, could never earn on our own. Jesus alone saves us. Read and explain Ephesians 2:8-9.

Jesus gives. Share with kids that Jesus lived a perfect life, died on the cross for our sins, and rose again. Because Jesus gave up His life for us, we can be welcomed into God's family for eternity. This is the best gift ever! Read Romans 5:8; 2 Corinthians 5:21; or 1 Peter 3:18.

We respond. Tell kids that they can respond to Jesus. Read Romans 10:9-10,13. Review these aspects of our response: Believe in your heart that Jesus alone saves you through what He's already done on the cross. Repent, turning from self and sin to Jesus. Tell God and others that your faith is in Jesus.

Offer to talk with any child who is interested in responding to Jesus. Provide *I'm a Christian Now!* for new Christians to take home and complete with their families.

APPLY the Story

SESSION TITLE: Living Like Jesus

BIBLE PASSAGE: 2 Peter 1

STORY POINT: Peter instructed believers to live like Jesus.

KEY PASSAGE: 2 Peter 1:3

BIG PICTURE QUESTION: How does the Holy Spirit help Christians? The Holy Spirit comforts us, shows us our sin, and guides us as we live for God's glory.

Key passage activity (5 minutes)

· Key Passage Poster

Invite volunteers to say the key passage from memory. Thank each kid for her efforts and encourage all the kids to continue working to memorize the key passage. Then direct the kids to stand in a circle. Say the first word of the key passage as you toss a tennis ball to another kid. When he catches the ball, he must say the next word and toss the ball to another kid, who will say the next word, and so on. Say the key passage multiple times in this way.

SAY • Peter wanted believers all over the world to know that even in hard times, we have everything we need to live like Jesus. God loves us and wants our lives to glorify Him. When we have the Holy Spirit, He helps us. *How does the Holy Spirit help Christians? The Holy Spirit comforts us, shows us our sin, and guides us as we live for God's glory.*

Discussion & Bible skills (10 minutes)

· Bibles, 1 per kid
· Story Point Poster
· Small Group Timeline and Map Set (005802970, optional)

Distribute a Bible to each kid. Help them find 2 Peter 1. Point out that the key passage comes from this chapter. Remind the kids that Peter was a fisherman from Galilee; the Holy Spirit made him into a church leader.

Ask the following questions. Lead the group to discuss:

Option: Retell or review the Bible story using the bolded text of the Bible story script.

1. What did Peter say God has given us? (*everything required for life and godliness, 2 Peter 1:3*)

2. What should we have along with faith? (*goodness, knowledge, self-control, endurance, godliness, brotherly affection; 2 Peter 1:5-7*)

3. Why did Peter want to remind believers of these things they already know? (*he knew he would soon die, and wanted to affirm the truth again before he did, 2 Peter 1:12-14*)

4. Why is it important to live for God? *Help kids think through the God's purpose for us. We were created to glorify and love Him. We cannot be truly happy apart from His plans for us. After faith in Jesus, our mission is to lead others to Jesus. If we say we love Jesus, and live as though we do not, our witness is ineffective.*

5. What are ways we can grow in godliness? *Guide kids to think about practical steps they can take to help them grow in their walk with Christ—such as reading their Bibles daily, gathering with other believers to learn about God, praying, and worshiping God. Remind kids that doing these things can't save them, but will help them grow in godliness if they are saved by grace through faith.*

6. Who does the work of growing us in godliness? *Discuss the combination between the Holy Spirit's power to change us, and our responsibility to live for God. Help kids see that we cannot change ourselves, but that with the Holy Spirit's power, we will be able to work towards loving and obeying God.*

SAY • **Peter instructed believers to live like Jesus**. We are called to live like Jesus too!

The Holy Spirit Empowers

83

- thank-you notes, 1 per kid
- pens or pencils

Tip: Use this activity option to reinforce the missions moment found in Teach the Story.

Activity choice (10 minutes)

OPTION 1: Thank-you notes

Distribute a thank-you note to each kid. Help the kids write thank-you notes to people who have helped them learn about Jesus, such as their parents, pastors, ministry volunteers, or missionaries your church supports.

SAY • Lottie Moon wrote many letters from China. She wrote encouraging people to give, to send more missionaries, and to pray. She also wrote to thank the people who supported her on her mission.

Each of us has been supported and loved in one way or another by people who want us to know more about Jesus and obey His commands. Don't forget to thank those who lived on mission so that you could know Jesus!

OPTION 2: Actions for words

- index cards
- pen

Write different simple nouns on index cards. Allow the kids to take turns drawing a card and acting out the noun without using any words or noises. Challenge the other kids to guess what word the volunteer is acting out.

Suggested nouns:
- cat
- baseball player
- dancer
- photographer
- bird

SAY • It was tough to guess those words based only on the actions. In a way, that reminds us of the lesson from today's story.

You may have heard the phrase "actions speak louder than words." If we say we love Jesus, our lives should show that. We live like Jesus so the world will see that He is our King. But actions with no words at all can be confusing as well. That's why we should not make the mistake of thinking that if we live like Jesus, we won't have to tell people about Him. Really living like Jesus means our whole lives are devoted to God's glory. That means our thoughts, speech, and actions all point to the gospel.

Reflection and prayer (5 minutes)

Distribute a sheet of paper to each child. Ask the kids to write about or draw a picture to answer the following questions:

- What does this story teach me about God or about the gospel?
- What does this story teach me about myself?
- Whom can I tell about this story?

Make sure to send the sheets home with kids alongside the activity page so that parents can see what their kids have been learning.

If time remains, take prayer requests or allow kids to complete the Bible story coloring page provided with this session. Pray for your group.

· pencils and crayons
· paper
· Bible Story Coloring Page, 1 per kid

Tip: Give parents this week's Big Picture Cards for Families to allow families to interact with the biblical content at home.

Unit 29: The Early Church

Unit Description:

The church is God's plan to bring praise and glory to Jesus. Through the church, the gospel goes beyond Jerusalem, Judea, and Samaria to the end of the earth. Even today, we are a part of God's mission to make sure everyone hears the gospel.

Key Passage:

Romans 12:5

Big Picture Question:

What is the church? The church is all Christians everywhere, who gather together in their communities to worship and serve God.

Session 1:

Ananias and Sapphira

Acts 4–5

Story Point: Ananias and Sapphira lied about their gift to the church.

Session 2:

Stephen's Sermon

Acts 6–7

Story Point: Stephen preached about Jesus no matter what.

Session 3:

The Good News

Romans 5–6

Story Point: God sent Jesus into the world to rescue sinners.

Session 4:

Doers of the Word

James 1–2

Story Point: James said that faith without works is useless.

Ananias and Sapphira

Ananias and Sapphira lied about their gift to the church.

Stephen's Sermon

Stephen preached about Jesus no matter what.

The Good News

God sent Jesus into the world to rescue sinners.

Doers of the Word

James said that faith without works is useless.

Unit 29 · Session 1
Ananias and Sapphira

BIBLE PASSAGE:
Acts 4–5

STORY POINT:
Ananias and Sapphira lied about their gift to the church.

KEY PASSAGE:
Romans 12:5

BIG PICTURE QUESTION:
What is the church? The church is all Christians everywhere, who gather together in their communities to worship and serve God.

INTRODUCE THE STORY (10–15 MINUTES) PAGE 92	TEACH THE STORY (25–30 MINUTES) PAGE 94	APPLY THE STORY (25–30 MINUTES) PAGE 100

Leaders, grow on the go! Listen to session-by-session training every week on Ministry Grid, Apple Podcasts, Spotify, or LifeWay's Digital Pass: ministrygrid.com/gospelproject | gospelproject.com/podcasts

LEADER Bible Study

Something amazing was happening among believers in the early church. Not only was the Holy Spirit changing people's hearts to believe in Jesus, He was empowering them to live differently. We see the evidence of God's grace among the believers in Acts 4:32-35. The believers shared everything they had. If one person had a need, someone else gladly gave what he had to meet that need. As a result, "there was not a needy person among them" (Acts 4:34).

Joseph (also known as Barnabas) was one of the disciples living in this way. He sold a field and gave the money to the apostles. But trouble arose when Ananias and his wife, Sapphira, sold some land. Perhaps they wanted to appear as generous as Barnabas without feeling the full cost of such generosity. They secretly kept back some of the money, and Ananias brought the rest to Peter.

When Peter confronted Ananias, he didn't tell him he was wrong to only bring part of the money. In fact, Peter said Ananias could have been honest about how the money was divided. Ananias and Sapphira's sin was in pretending to be generous when they were actually greedy. They had tried to deceive the apostles, but Peter pointed out that they were guilty of trying to deceive God. Ananias dropped dead, and a few hours later his wife did too.

As you teach this story to kids, avoid using Ananias and Sapphira as a warning to be generous or die. As sinners, we struggle with the temptation of greed. Point kids to Jesus, who forgives our greed and changes us through the Holy Spirit. The Holy Spirit changes our hearts to want to share with those in need because Jesus generously gave all He had so we can share in His riches and have forgiveness and eternal life.

The **BIBLE** Story

Ananias and Sapphira
Acts 4–5

The early church was growing. By the power of the Holy Spirit, the apostles were telling people that Jesus had been raised from the dead. **A large group of believers met together in Jerusalem. They shared everything they had.** If someone had more than he needed, he gladly gave it away so everyone had what he needed.

One man, Barnabas, sold a field and gave the money to the apostles. The apostles used the money to help people in need. Everyone who had land or houses did the same. **Ananias and his wife, Sapphira, sold some land and pretended to give all of the money to the apostles,** but they kept some of it for themselves.

When Ananias brought the money to the apostles, **Peter asked him, "Why are you lying to the Holy Spirit? You could have been honest about what you did with the money, but instead you lied—not to us, but to God." When Ananias heard this, he** fell down, **died,** and was buried. Everyone who heard about this was filled with fear.

About three hours later, **Sapphira came to the apostles.** She did not know what had happened to her husband. **Peter asked her, "Is this all** the money you got for the land?"

"Yes," she said. "That's all of it."

Peter said, "Why did you and your husband agree to test the Lord?" Then Sapphira fell dead too. Great fear came on everyone in the church and all who heard about these things.

Christ Connection: Ananias and Sapphira wanted to look generous, but they were greedy. The Holy Spirit changes our hearts to want to share with those in need because Jesus generously gave all He had so we can share in His riches and have forgiveness and eternal life.

Bible Storytelling Tips

- **Doodle it:** Draw simple shapes and diagrams to help you tell the story.
- **Act it out:** Use kid volunteers to act out the story as you tell it.

INTRODUCE the Story

SESSION TITLE: Ananias and Sapphira

BIBLE PASSAGE: Acts 4–5

STORY POINT: Ananias and Sapphira lied about their gift to the church.

KEY PASSAGE: Romans 12:5

BIG PICTURE QUESTION: What is the church? The church is all Christians everywhere, who gather together in their communities to worship and serve God.

Welcome time

Greet each kid as he or she arrives. Use this time to collect the offering, fill out attendance sheets, and help new kids connect to your group. Prompt kids to discuss a time they did something generous.

SAY • Generosity is a wonderful character trait. God is generous toward us. He gives us wonderful gifts, the most incredible of which is Jesus. Today we will learn about two people who wanted to seem very generous without being very generous.

Activity page (5 minutes)

- "Spot the Differences" activity page, 1 per kid
- pencils or markers

Invite kids to complete the "Spot the Differences" activity page. Kids will search the two versions of the Bible story picture, looking for seven differences between the two.

SAY • Telling the difference between a person who is truly generous and a person who only wants to seem generous can be tricky. Today we will learn about a man and his wife who only wanted to seem generous. They tried to hide money, and lied about it. Do you think you can trick God with a lie? Of course not! He knows everything. We'll learn more soon.

Session starter (10 minutes)

LOW PREP

OPTION 1: Two facts and a fiction

Instruct the kids to sit in a circle. Select a kid to start the game by making three statements about themselves. Two of them must be true, and one must be false. The other kids must determine which statement is not true. Continue playing until each kid has a chance to offer three statements.

SAY • In a fun game, we might say something untrue to be silly or entertain one another. Today, we will learn about two people who wanted to seem very generous without behaving very generously. They told a lie to trick church leaders.

OPTION 2: Hide the coin

Ask the kids to stand in a circle. Select one kid to stand in the middle. Instruct the other kids to place their hands behind their back, holding them open. Tell all kids to close their eyes. Walk around the circle and secretly place a plastic coin into one kid's hands. Instruct the kids to open their eyes. The kid in the middle must determine who is hiding the coin.

· plastic coin

SAY • It was tricky to figure out who was hiding the coin. Today we will learn about a time two people tried to hide money from the church. They said they were giving all they earned even though they were only giving some. We will talk more about it soon.

Transition to teach the story

TEACH the Story

SESSION TITLE: Ananias and Sapphira
BIBLE PASSAGE: Acts 4–5
STORY POINT: Ananias and Sapphira lied about their gift to the church.
KEY PASSAGE: Romans 12:5
BIG PICTURE QUESTION: What is the church? The church is all Christians everywhere, who gather together in their communities to worship and serve God.

· room decorations
· Theme Background Slide (optional)

Suggested Theme Decorating Ideas: Cover a table with a black tablecloth. Use desk lamp and magnifying glass to set up a station where a coin collector might examin and evaluate coins. Hang posters of coins and minting information, and place a coin collector's guide on the table.

Countdown

· countdown video

Show the countdown video as you transition to teach the story. Set it to end as the session begins.

Introduce the session (3 minutes)

· leader attire

[Leader enters wearing nice clothing and white gloves.]
LEADER • Oh, hello there! I wasn't expecting this many coin collectors at my presentation. Don't mistake me, I'm very glad you are all here. I love teaching people about coin collecting nearly as much as I love coin collecting itself. There's something so satisfying about seeing someone else fall in love with the hobby I have found thrilling for all these years. Very little compares to the wonderful feeling of finding a rare and valuable coin from the past. Even so, I can definitely think of a few things that are better.

For example, the joy of loving Jesus and teaching

Tip: If you prefer not to use themed content or characters, adapt or omit this introduction.

others about Him is definitely better than coin collecting. I especially love when I can use my love of coins to tell someone about my even greater love for Jesus. Did you know that the church is kind of like a coin collection? Lots of different kinds of coins come together to make an interesting and valuable collection. In a similar way, God brings lots of people together to make His wonderful church.

Big picture question (1 minute)

LEADER • But *what is the church?* It's not a building, though sometimes people speak as though it is. *The church is all Christians everywhere, who gather together in their communities to worship and serve God.* That means the church is people! People who love God and want to obey Him. There are local churches who gather together in specific communities where the members live, and there's also the global church, which is every single believer across the world—and even throughout history!

Giant timeline (1 minute)

Show the giant timeline. Point to individual Bible stories as you review.

· Giant Timeline

LEADER • Speaking of the church throughout history, we have been learning about the very early days of Jesus' church. The Holy Spirit came to live with believers, and right away they began preaching the good news and living on mission. They gave generously, worshiped God, took care of the poor, and taught others how to obey God. But the early church had some problems too. Let's hear a story about that.

The Early Church

Tell the Bible story (10 minutes)

- Bibles
- "Ananias and Sapphira" video
- Big Picture Question Poster
- Bible Story Picture Poster
- Story Point Poster

Open your Bible to Acts 4–5. Use the Bible storytelling tips on the Bible story page to help you tell the story, or show the Bible story video "Ananias and Sapphira."

LEADER • There are two main ideas I want us to think about from that story: how Ananias and Sapphira sinned, and what it means to fear God.

Ananias and Sapphira were not sinning by keeping some of the money from the land they sold. Peter even told them the money was theirs to do with what they wanted. Their sin was lying about the money they gave. They said they were giving all the money from their land, while secretly keeping some of it for themselves.

That brings us to the next idea: What does it mean to fear God? When the Bible speaks about fearing God, it's not the kind of fear you might be thinking of, where you dislike something and don't want to go near it ever. Fear of the Lord is about understanding His power and holiness.

We fear the Lord when we love and respect Him, and desire to honor Him with our lives. God is powerful and hates sin; people who try to oppose Him will fail and be separated from Him. God will protect His people from their enemies. Fearing God means understanding how dangerous it is to be an enemy of God. Fearing God means we want to be His children by having faith in Jesus. Ananias and Sapphira lied to God, and their deaths spread fear of God through the early church, strengthening believers.

Christ connection

LEADER • Ananias and Sapphira wanted to look generous, but they were greedy. The Holy Spirit changes our hearts to want to share with those in need because Jesus generously gave all He had so we can share in His riches and have forgiveness and eternal life.

Giving generously is an honor and a great source of joy. God isn't interested in forcing us to give away money that we don't want to give away. God wants us to see the beauty of His generosity and understand that He will provide for all our needs. God wants us to be generous as the Holy Spirit grows us to be more like Jesus. Our generosity should come from our love of God and our desire to see His mission fulfilled.

Note: You may use this opportunity to use Scripture and the guide provided to explain how to become a Christian. Make sure kids know when and where they can ask questions.

Questions from kids video (3 minutes)

Show the "Unit 29, Session 1" questions from kids video. Prompt kids to think about how the church uses money given in offerings. Guide them to discuss how they feel about giving money to the church.

· "Unit 29, Session 1" Questions from Kids video

 ## Missions moment (3 minutes)

Play the "All About the Twin Cities" missions video.

LEADER • The first churches had a lot to learn about how to honor Jesus and do right by others. **Ananias and Sapphira lied about their gift to the church**. They needed the Holy Spirit to change their hearts so that they would do what is right. For the next few sessions, we're going to learn about two cities in the U.S. that need more churches and Christians who will help the people living there know Jesus.

· "Partner with Twin Cities" missions video

The Early Church

Key passage (5 minutes)

· Key Passage Poster
· "We Who Are Many (Romans 12:5)" song

Show the key passage poster. Lead the boys and girls to read together Romans 12:5. Then sing the key passage song.

LEADER • Paul's letter to the Roman believers contains one of the most clear explanations of the gospel. Our key passage comes near the end of the Book of Romans, where Paul reminds believers what it means to be part of the church. The church is united as one body, working together for God's glory and our good. Even though individuals are all created uniquely by God to be wonderful and special creations, we all work together as one church.

Sing (4 minutes)

· "One Foundation" song

LEADER • God is good to us. He generously sent Jesus to rescue us from sin and provide the foundation we need to build our lives on.

Sing together "One Foundation"

Pray (2 minutes)

Invite kids to pray before dismissing to apply the story.

LEADER • Father, thank You for all You do for us. Help us to fear You and draw near to You. Give us generous hearts that want to see Your mission accomplished in the world. Amen.

Dismiss to apply the story

The Gospel: God's Plan for Me

Ask kids if they have ever heard the word *gospel*. Clarify that the word *gospel* means "good news." It is the message about Christ, the kingdom of God, and salvation. Use the following guide to share the gospel with kids.

God rules. Explain to kids that the Bible tells us God created everything, and He is in charge of everything. Invite a volunteer to read Genesis 1:1 from the Bible. Read Revelation 4:11 or Colossians 1:16-17 aloud and explain what these verses mean.

We sinned. Tell kids that since the time of Adam and Eve, everyone has chosen to disobey God. (Romans 3:23) The Bible calls this sin. Because God is holy, God cannot be around sin. Sin separates us from God and deserves God's punishment of death. (Romans 6:23)

God provided. Choose a child to read John 3:16 aloud. Say that God sent His Son, Jesus, the perfect solution to our sin problem, to rescue us from the punishment we deserve. It's something we, as sinners, could never earn on our own. Jesus alone saves us. Read and explain Ephesians 2:8-9.

Jesus gives. Share with kids that Jesus lived a perfect life, died on the cross for our sins, and rose again. Because Jesus gave up His life for us, we can be welcomed into God's family for eternity. This is the best gift ever! Read Romans 5:8; 2 Corinthians 5:21; or 1 Peter 3:18.

We respond. Tell kids that they can respond to Jesus. Read Romans 10:9-10,13. Review these aspects of our response: Believe in your heart that Jesus alone saves you through what He's already done on the cross. Repent, turning from self and sin to Jesus. Tell God and others that your faith is in Jesus.

Offer to talk with any child who is interested in responding to Jesus. Provide *I'm a Christian Now!* for new Christians to take home and complete with their families.

The Early Church

APPLY the Story

SESSION TITLE: Ananias and Sapphira

BIBLE PASSAGE: Acts 4–5

STORY POINT: Ananias and Sapphira lied about their gift to the church.

KEY PASSAGE: Romans 12:5

BIG PICTURE QUESTION: What is the church? The church is all Christians everywhere, who gather together in their communities to worship and serve God.

Key passage activity (5 minutes)

- Key Passage Poster
- index cards
- markers

Write each word of the key passage on a separate index card. Read the key passage through a few times with the kids. Then shuffle the cards and challenge the kids to put them in the right order. Play again as time allows.

SAY • God wants Christians to live together in community, loving and supporting one another. This key passage, from Paul's letter to believers in Rome, helps us remember that truth. The church is made up of individual Christians, but we need one another in the same way a healthy body needs all the individual parts of a body. *What is the church? The church is all Christians everywhere, who gather together in their communities to worship and serve God.*

Discussion & Bible skills (10 minutes)

- Bibles, 1 per kid
- Story Point Poster
- Small Group Timeline and Map Set (005802970, optional)

Distribute a Bible to each kid. Help them find Acts 4–5. Remind the kids that Acts is in the History division of the New Testament. It is the only book in that division. Explain that Acts was written by Luke, who also wrote the Gospel of Luke. In some ways, Acts is like the sequel to all the gospels but especially to the Gospel of Luke.

Ask the following questions. Lead the group to discuss:

1. Who sold his land and gave all the money to the church? (*Joseph, also called Barnabas; Acts 4:36-37*)
2. When Ananias and Sapphira sold their land, did they give all the money? (*No, Acts 5:1-2*)
3. Why did Ananias and Sapphira die? (*They lied to God, Acts 5:3-4, 8-9*)
4. Why does God want us to give money to the church? *Help kids see that God doesn't need our money. Remind them that all of creation belongs to Him. He created us and needs nothing from us. Help them see that God's desire for us is to experience the joy that comes from generous giving. He allows us to be a part of His wonderful mission to save sinners, and He wants us to be cheerful in the way we participate, including by giving generously.*
5. What are some ways we can give generously? *Guide kids to think beyond just giving money. Help them think about ways they can give time or talent by serving the church. Explain that generosity is not about the amount you give but the attitude of your heart when you give.*
6. Do you think we should give even if we don't want to? *Encourage kids to answer this question honestly. Remind kids that sometimes the act of giving can help change our hearts to want to give. Help them see that refusal to give usually reveals sin in their hearts, even though not giving isn't itself sinful.*

SAY • **Ananias and Sapphira lied about their gift to the church.** They wanted to appear generous without actually allowing the Holy Spirit to make them generous. Giving doesn't save us, and we don't have to give; but when we love God, He helps us want to.

Option: Retell or review the Bible story using the bolded text of the Bible story script.

Activity choice (10 minutes)

OPTION 1: Clothing drive

Guide kids to wrap the boxes and decorate them for a clothes drive at your church to collect hats and gloves for a homeless shelter in your city or a clothes closet at a church. If you live in a city that is warm in the winter, collect other appropriate clothing like new t-shirts or toiletry supplies. Talk with your church staff about the best places in the church to put the collection boxes. Encourage kids to bring items for the boxes. If possible, arrange for kids to go with you later in the month to deliver the items.

Tip: Use this activity option to reinforce the missions moment found in Teach the Story.

SAY • Winters in the Twin Cities of Minneapolis and St. Paul, Minnesota can be very cold and snowy. People who don't have adequate protection from the cold can be in real danger when the temperature drops. Churches there collect warm clothing to give to people who need coats and gloves.

We can live on mission by providing for the people who live near us too! We can collect the gear that people need here to get through the winter.

OPTION 2: Have to or want to?

Designate one side of the room as "Have to" and the other side of the room as "Want to." You may choose to make signs and hang them to help kids remember the two options. Give the kids actions they could take and ask them to move to the side of the room that represents how they feel about the given action; do they have to do it? Or would they want to?

LOW PREP

· paper (optional)
· marker (optional)
· tape (optional)

Suggested actions:
  • clean your room
  • eat a candy bar

- wash dishes
- fold laundry
- play a game with your friends
- give generously to others
- obey God

SAY • **Ananias and Sapphira lied about their gift to the church.** They probably thought of giving money as something they had to do to seem generous. They didn't see it as something they wanted to do out of love for God and the church.

Sometimes we have to do things we may not want to do, like chores or schoolwork. When it comes to obeying God, the Holy Spirit fills the hearts of believers to change them from the inside out. We don't just *have* to obey God; we get to! Obeying God is an honor. His plans are perfect, and even though He doesn't need us for them to work out, He chooses to use us!

Reflection and prayer (5 minutes)

Distribute a sheet of paper to each child. Ask the kids to write about or draw a picture to answer the following questions:

- What does this story teach me about God or about the gospel?
- What does this story teach me about myself?
- Whom can I tell about this story?

Make sure to send the sheets home with kids alongside the activity page so that parents can see what their kids have been learning.

If time remains, take prayer requests or allow kids to complete the Bible story coloring page provided with this session. Pray for your group.

· pencils and crayons
· paper
· Bible Story Coloring Page, 1 per kid

Tip: Give parents this week's Big Picture Cards for Families to allow families to interact with the biblical content at home.

The Early Church

Use Week of:

Unit 29 · Session 2
Stephen's Sermon

BIBLE PASSAGE:
Acts 6–7

STORY POINT:
Stephen preached about Jesus no matter what.

KEY PASSAGE:
Romans 12:5

BIG PICTURE QUESTION:
What is the church? The church is all Christians everywhere, who gather together in their communities to worship and serve God.

INTRODUCE THE STORY
(10–15 MINUTES)
PAGE 108

→

TEACH THE STORY
(25–30 MINUTES)
PAGE 110

→

APPLY THE STORY
(25–30 MINUTES)
PAGE 116

Leaders, grow on the go! Listen to session-by-session training every week on Ministry Grid, Apple Podcasts, Spotify, or LifeWay's Digital Pass: ministrygrid.com/gospelproject | gospelproject.com/podcasts

LEADER Bible Study

Stephen was one of the seven men chosen to serve as leaders in the early church at Jerusalem. (See Acts 6:1-7.) God blessed Stephen and gave him power to do wonders and miracles like some of the apostles.

Some of the Jews accused Stephen of blasphemy and dragged him to the Sanhedrin, a group of Jewish leaders who acted as a legal council. Stephen addressed the group. He drew from the Jewish history, which the leaders of the Sanhedrin would have known well. But Stephen taught from the Old Testament things the Jewish leaders had likely never realized.

As Stephen preached, he showed how the Old Testament pointed to a coming Savior and how that Savior was Jesus. Stephen pointed out that the Jews' ancestors had rejected God's prophets. And they were just like their fathers; they rejected the Messiah, the Lord Jesus. Not only did they reject Jesus, they killed Him!

The Jewish leaders rushed at Stephen. As he faced his enemies, Stephen looked into heaven and saw God's glory. Jesus was standing at God's right hand. The Jews forced Stephen out of the city, and they stoned him.

Remind kids of Jesus' words in Matthew 10:22: "You will be hated by everyone because of my name. But the one who endures to the end will be saved." Following Jesus will include difficulty and suffering. Jesus gives words of both warning and comfort: "Don't be afraid" (Matt. 10:26).

Stephen was killed because he was a Christian. Jesus told His followers that they would be persecuted—hated, hurt, or even killed—for loving Him. (Mark 13:9-13; John 16:2) Jesus also said that those who suffer for Him would be blessed. (Matt. 5:11) Stephen was not afraid to die because he saw Jesus waiting for him in heaven. We can face suffering in this life because we know great joy is waiting for us in heaven.

The **BIBLE** Story

Stephen's Sermon

Acts 6–7

Stephen was one of Jesus' followers. **God** blessed Stephen and **gave him power to do great wonders and signs.** One day, **some Jews began to argue with Stephen. The Holy Spirit helped Stephen speak with wisdom,** so no matter how hard the Jews tried, they could not win the argument.

The Jews lied about Stephen; they said he had spoken against God. **The people dragged Stephen to** the Sanhedrin (san HEE drihn), **the Jewish court, and told more lies**. "We heard Stephen say that Jesus will destroy the temple and change the laws that Moses gave us," they said.

"Is this true?" the high priest asked Stephen.

Stephen began to preach about Jesus. He reminded the court about Abraham. God had made promises to Abraham and his son Isaac. **He reminded them about** Joseph and **Moses.** God kept Joseph safe when his brothers tried to hurt him, and God used Joseph to help all His people during a famine. When God's people lived in Egypt, God called Moses to rescue His people from Pharaoh. **Moses led God's people away from Egypt, but they turned against Moses and against God. God did not give up on His people, though.** He was working out a plan. **God worked**

through Joshua and David and Solomon.

The religious leaders knew these stories from the Old Testament. **Stephen told them these stories to explain that Jesus was the Messiah God had promised!** But just like their ancestors rejected and killed the prophets in the Old Testament, these Jewish leaders had rejected Jesus and murdered Him!

Stephen's words made the Jewish leaders so angry! Stephen was filled with the Holy Spirit. He looked up to heaven and saw Jesus standing there.

"Look!" he said. "I see the heavens opened and the Son of Man standing at the right hand of God!"

The Jewish leaders screamed at the top of their lungs. They **covered their ears and rushed at Stephen. They threw him out of the city and began throwing stones at him. Stephen called out,** "Lord Jesus, receive my spirit!" Then he said, **"Lord, do not hold this sin against them!" After this, Stephen died.**

Christ Connection: Stephen was killed because he was a Christian. Jesus told His followers that they would be persecuted—hated, hurt, or even killed—for loving Him. Jesus also said that those who suffer for Him would be blessed. We can face suffering in this life because Jesus suffered first. He died and then rose again, and He is waiting for us in heaven.

Bible Storytelling Tips

- **Set up stations:** place stools around the room, each with a prop to help you tell the story, such as a bible, a pyramid, a stone, and so forth.
- **Use the timeline:** As you speak about the different parts of Israel's history, use the Giant Timeline to point out the Bible story art from those stories.

INTRODUCE the Story

SESSION TITLE: Stephen's Sermon
BIBLE PASSAGE: Acts 6–7
STORY POINT: Stephen preached about Jesus no matter what.
KEY PASSAGE: Romans 12:5
BIG PICTURE QUESTION: What is the church? The church is all Christians everywhere, who gather together in their communities to worship and serve God.

Welcome time

Greet each kid as he or she arrives. Use this time to collect the offering, fill out attendance sheets, and help new kids connect to your group. Prompt kids to tell stories about times they spoke in front of a group. Perhaps they had to make a presentation at school, or had a speaking part in a church play.

SAY • Speaking in front of others can feel a little scary to some. Today we will learn about a man whom God used to preach a message to religious leaders who hated the message of Jesus. How do you think they reacted? We'll learn more soon.

Activity page (5 minutes)

· "Learn From the Past" activity page, 1 per kid
· pencils or markers

Tip: Use the Small Group Timeline and Map Set (005802970) to help kids remember which stories came first.

Invite kids to complete the "Learn From the Past" activity page. Challenge kids to number in chronological order the people from past Bible stories.

SAY • Great job putting those people in the right order. Each one of those people had a part to play in God's plan to send Jesus and save the world from sin. Today we will learn about a man named Stephen who used stories from the past to help explain the gospel.

Younger Kids Leader Guide
Unit 29 • Session 2

Session starter (10 minutes)

OPTION 1: The great debate

LOW PREP

Provide the group with two opposing options, such as whether they like tacos or pizza better. Form two teams based on who selects which option. Challenge each team to provide reasoning and evidence to explain why their choice is the better choice. Can any of the kids convince others to change teams?

SAY • Something like a favorite food or favorite game to play isn't particularly important. We can all have a different opinion, and no one is wrong. However, something like whether or not Jesus is God's Son, who died on the cross for sin and rose on the third day? Whether you agree with that is super important. Today we will learn about a time Stephen preached to convince religious leaders that Jesus is the Messiah.

OPTION 2: Right hand man

Challenge kids to complete a task—such as drawing a simple figure, writing their name, or tossing and catching a ball—using only their left hands. Then ask them to do the same challenge using their right hands. Compare the results of both.

· paper (optional)
· pencils (optional)
· rubber balls (optional)

SAY • It's tough to complete tasks with your non-dominant hand! The majority of people in the world are right-handed. As a result, it is often considered a great honor to be at someone's right hand. Someone's "right hand" man or woman is their most trusted helper or advisor. Did you know Jesus is at God the Father's right hand? Let's learn more about that.

Transition to teach the story

TEACH the Story

SESSION TITLE: Stephen's Sermon
BIBLE PASSAGE: Acts 6–7
STORY POINT: Stephen preached about Jesus no matter what.
KEY PASSAGE: Romans 12:5
BIG PICTURE QUESTION: What is the church? The church is all Christians everywhere, who gather together in their communities to worship and serve God.

Countdown

· countdown video

Show the countdown video as you transition to teach the story. Set it to end as the session begins.

Introduce the session (3 minutes)

· leader attire

[Leader enters wearing nice clothing and white gloves.]

LEADER • Hey everyone! Welcome back to my coin collection class. Try saying that three times fast! One of the best parts of coin collecting is figuring out which coins you don't have yet, and planning ways to get those coins into your collection.

Tip: If you prefer not to use themed content or characters, adapt or omit this introduction.

Over the last five months, I've been searching everywhere for a 1995 double die penny. They are quite rare and worth a lot more than one cent. You see, when a coin is made, they use a strong metal pattern called a die to literally slam down and stamp the imprint of the coin design onto a disc of metal—called a blank.

Sometimes, that die hits the blank, bounces slightly, and hits a second time. That's what "double die" means. You can recognize a double die coin because you will notice the pattern stamped onto the coin twice, very slightly overlapping. It leads to a blurry or poorly defined looking coin at a glance. Interesting that sometimes the most valuable coins are the ones that turned out wrong, isn't it?

Well, just as a coin collector is often interested even in the "broken" coins, God wants everyone to believe the gospel, even those who seem furthest from Him. This week, we will hear a story about a man named Stephen sharing the gospel with others who hated the message so much, they attacked him.

Big picture question (1 minute)

LEADER • As we get into the story, let's remember our big picture question and answer. *What is the church? The church is all Christians everywhere, who gather together in their communities to worship and serve God.* That means that the church is people. Local churches are groups of believers who gather in their cities or neighborhoods, and the global church is all Christians all over the world. Individual believers make up one united church, and our goal is to glorify God, care for one another, and spread the good news to new people so the church will grow.

Giant timeline (1 minute)

Show the giant timeline. Point to individual Bible stories as you review.

· Giant Timeline

LEADER • Last week we talked about the early church's generosity toward one another, and learned that **Ananias and Sapphira lied about their gift to the church**. When they died, fear of the Lord spread

The Early Church

and the church was stronger as a result. This week we will learn about another man who died. But his death was for a very different reason, and God used it for good in a very different way. Our story is called "Stephen's Sermon."

Tell the Bible story (10 minutes)

Open your Bible to Acts 6–7. Use the Bible storytelling tips on the Bible story page to help you tell the story, or show the Bible story video "Stephen's Sermon."

LEADER • The men Stephen preached to needed Jesus to save them from their sin, but they did not want to believe the truth. They refused to accept that they needed a savior or that Jesus was the Savior God had promised. They hated the truth so much, they killed Stephen to try and keep people from hearing it. Even so, Stephen asked God to forgive them.

Stephen preached about Jesus no matter what, even when it cost him his life. He cared more about giving lost people the opportunity to have faith in Jesus and be saved than he did about his own safety. Stephen's death is a reminder of Jesus' death. Jesus allowed the religious leaders and the Romans to crucify Him so that He could be the perfect sacrifice for sin, and the one way for us to be reunited with God.

After Stephen was murdered, the believers living in Jerusalem began to scatter. They left their homes to escape persecution, but they carried their faith with them. They spread the gospel further than it had been before. God used Stephen's death to strengthen and grow His church.

- Bibles
- "Stephen's Sermon" video
- Big Picture Question Poster
- Bible Story Picture Poster
- Story Point Poster

Christ connection

LEADER • Stephen was killed because he was a Christian. Jesus told His followers that they would be persecuted—hated, hurt, or even killed—for loving Him. Jesus also said that those who suffer for Him would be blessed. We can face suffering in this life because Jesus suffered first. He died and then rose again, and He is waiting for us in heaven.

Note: You may use this opportunity to use Scripture and the guide provided to explain how to become a Christian. Make sure kids know when and where they can ask questions.

Questions from kids video (3 minutes)

Show the "Unit 29, Session 2" questions from kids video. Prompt kids to think about who in their families may need to hear the gospel. Guide them to discuss who first shared the gospel with them.

· "Unit 29, Session 2" Questions from Kids video

Missions moment (3 minutes)

Display the "Nache Photos" printable. Select strong readers to help you read the captions.

LEADER • Stephen told other people about Jesus even though it cost him his life. Some of the people who come to the Nache's church understand what it means to live in danger. The Naches want the people to know about Jesus and to be bold about following Him, even if others in their community don't believe.

· "Nache Photos" printable

Key passage (5 minutes)

Show the key passage poster. Lead the boys and girls to read together Romans 12:5. Then sing the key passage song.

LEADER • Paul wrote these words to the church in Rome. He wanted them to know that, even though many different and diverse people make up the church, the church is united by Jesus. We are one body and

· Key Passage Poster
· "We Who Are Many (Romans 12:5)" song

Jesus is the head. He leads us, and without Him, the church would not exist. That's why we worship and serve Him together.

Sing (4 minutes)

· "One Foundation" song

LEADER • Paul also describes the church like a building, and Jesus is our perfect foundation on which the church is built. He keeps us strong and helps us stand up for the truth of His gospel.

Sing together "One Foundation."

Pray (2 minutes)

Invite kids to pray before dismissing to apply the story.

LEADER • Father, thank You that even our darkest moments can be used by You for good. Help us trust You even in hard times. Give us courage to preach the gospel as Stephen did, no matter what. Amen.

Dismiss to apply the story

The Gospel: God's Plan for Me

Ask kids if they have ever heard the word *gospel*. Clarify that the word *gospel* means "good news." It is the message about Christ, the kingdom of God, and salvation. Use the following guide to share the gospel with kids.

God rules. Explain to kids that the Bible tells us God created everything, and He is in charge of everything. Invite a volunteer to read Genesis 1:1 from the Bible. Read Revelation 4:11 or Colossians 1:16-17 aloud and explain what these verses mean.

We sinned. Tell kids that since the time of Adam and Eve, everyone has chosen to disobey God. (Romans 3:23) The Bible calls this sin. Because God is holy, God cannot be around sin. Sin separates us from God and deserves God's punishment of death. (Romans 6:23)

God provided. Choose a child to read John 3:16 aloud. Say that God sent His Son, Jesus, the perfect solution to our sin problem, to rescue us from the punishment we deserve. It's something we, as sinners, could never earn on our own. Jesus alone saves us. Read and explain Ephesians 2:8-9.

Jesus gives. Share with kids that Jesus lived a perfect life, died on the cross for our sins, and rose again. Because Jesus gave up His life for us, we can be welcomed into God's family for eternity. This is the best gift ever! Read Romans 5:8; 2 Corinthians 5:21; or 1 Peter 3:18.

We respond. Tell kids that they can respond to Jesus. Read Romans 10:9-10,13. Review these aspects of our response: Believe in your heart that Jesus alone saves you through what He's already done on the cross. Repent, turning from self and sin to Jesus. Tell God and others that your faith is in Jesus.

Offer to talk with any child who is interested in responding to Jesus. Provide *I'm a Christian Now!* for new Christians to take home and complete with their families.

APPLY the Story

SESSION TITLE: Stephen's Sermon

BIBLE PASSAGE: Acts 6–7

STORY POINT: Stephen preached about Jesus no matter what.

KEY PASSAGE: Romans 12:5

BIG PICTURE QUESTION: What is the church? The church is all Christians everywhere, who gather together in their communities to worship and serve God.

Key passage activity (5 minutes)

· Key Passage Poster

Instruct the kids to stand in a circle. Tell kids to stand on one leg and begin saying the key passage in unison. If anyone wobbles and puts their foot down, stop the group and start them over from the beginning. Challenge the kids to see how many times they can say the key passage while balancing on one leg.

SAY • Surprisingly, it can be tough to do something as simple as balancing on one foot if you are occupying your brain with something like remembering something you have memorized. It doesn't take much to make our bodies struggle to work together! Paul knew that was true about the body of Christ too, so he wrote our key passage to remind believers that they should be united as one in Jesus.

Discussion & Bible skills (10 minutes)

· Bibles, 1 per kid
· Story Point Poster
· Small Group Timeline and Map Set (005802970, optional)

Distribute a Bible to each kid. Help them find Acts 6–7. Remind them that Acts is the only book in the History division of the New Testament. Ask kids if they know who wrote Acts. (*Luke*) Consider pointing out Jerusalem on the New Testament Israel Map. (*H5*)

Ask the following questions. Lead the group to discuss:

Option: Retell or review the Bible story using the bolded text of the Bible story script.

1. What was Stephen accused of? (*blasphemy, saying something untrue and dishonoring about God; Acts 6:11*)
2. What did Stephen preach about? (*Stephen used Israel's history to explain Jesus is the Messiah; Acts 7:51-52*)
3. What did the religious leaders do to Stephen as a result of his preaching about Jesus? (*killed him, Acts 7:57-60*)
4. Have you ever faced persecution for your faith? *Guide kids to think about ways they may feel persecuted. Be sensitive to their experiences while taking care not to minimize the harsh persecution Christians face in other parts of the world.*
5. How can we stand up boldly for Jesus in the face of persecution? *Discuss the strength and power available to believers through the Holy Spirit. Remind kids that He can help us be bold in hard times. Encourage kids to trust God and have faith that He turns all things to good, even when we don't see the good results.*
6. What should we do if we are persecuted? *Talk through what Stephen did. Help the kids see that Stephen did not fight his enemies, but instead asked God to forgive them for killing him. Remind kids that Jesus promised troubles and persecution would come. Encourage kids to pray for boldness in hard times, not just for things to get easier.*

SAY • **Stephen preached about Jesus no matter what.** We may not face the same kind of persecution. But whatever we face, trusting God is the best option. We can pray for boldness in the face of persecution and that God will use our trials to bless His church.

Activity choice (10 minutes)

OPTION 1: Naches on mission

Ask a volunteer to find Minnesota on a US map. Point out Minneapolis and St. Paul. Explain that the two cities are very close to each other.

Show the "Nache Photos" printable again. Form three small groups and give each group one photo. Ask each group to think of three ways to pray for the Naches and their work to start churches in Minneapolis.

SAY • Many immigrants from Africa come to Minneapolis and St. Paul. Since the Naches also came to the US from Africa, they are uniquely gifted to share Christ with the immigrants. They understand what it's like to come to a new city.

We can live on mission like the Naches by seeking ways to share the truth of God with people around us who may not know Him. Sometimes, preaching the gospel may cost us; others may dislike us because of our faith, but we know that we can stand firm for the gospel because of the Holy Spirit in us.

OPTION 2: Upgrade

Place a variety of items around the room. Provide the kids with paper and pencils. Instruct the kids to list the items least to most valuable. Encourage the kids to think about more than just the price, but also how much they would want to own or use each item. Compare different kids' lists.

Suggested items: playground ball, candy, bicycle, first aid kit, action figure, baby doll.

SAY • For some of you, trading one of those items for another might be an easy choice. You might see it as an upgrade to give up a playground ball to get a

LOW PREP

· US map
· "Nache Photos" printable

Tip: Use this activity option to reinforce the missions moment found in Teach the Story.

· variety of items (playground ball, candy, bicycle, first aid kit, action figure, baby doll, etc.)

bicycle. In a way, that helps us think about our the choices Stephen made in our story today.

What did Stephen give up? [*His life.*] What did Stephen gain? [*He got to be with Jesus in heaven, he got to stand up for the truth, he got to be a part of God's plan to spread the gospel, and so forth.*] Stephen understood that Jesus is more valuable than anything, even our lives! For believers, even death is an upgrade because we get to be with Jesus forever.

Reflection and prayer (5 minutes)

Distribute a sheet of paper to each child. Ask the kids to write about or draw a picture to answer the following questions:

- What does this story teach me about God or about the gospel?
- What does this story teach me about myself?
- Whom can I tell about this story?

Make sure to send the sheets home with kids alongside the activity page so that parents can see what their kids have been learning.

If time remains, take prayer requests or allow kids to complete the Bible story coloring page provided with this session. Pray for your group.

· pencils and crayons
· paper
· Bible Story Coloring Page, 1 per kid

Tip: Give parents this week's Big Picture Cards for Families to allow families to interact with the biblical content at home.

Use Week of:

Unit 29 · Session 3
The Good News

BIBLE PASSAGE:
Romans 5–6

STORY POINT:
God sent Jesus into the world to rescue sinners.

KEY PASSAGE:
Romans 12:5

BIG PICTURE QUESTION:
What is the church? The church is all Christians everywhere, who gather together in their communities to worship and serve God.

INTRODUCE THE STORY
(10–15 MINUTES)
PAGE 124

→

TEACH THE STORY
(25–30 MINUTES)
PAGE 126

→

APPLY THE STORY
(25–30 MINUTES)
PAGE 132

Leaders, grow on the go! Listen to session-by-session training every week on Ministry Grid, Apple Podcasts, Spotify, or LifeWay's Digital Pass:
ministrygrid.com/gospelproject | gospelproject.com/podcasts

Younger Kids Leader Guide
Unit 29 • Session 3

LEADER Bible Study

After Jesus returned to heaven and sent the Holy Spirit to the apostles, the gospel began to spread. Those who heard the good news at Pentecost included visitors from Rome, and they were likely among the three thousand who believed. (See Acts 2:10,41.) When Paul wrote his letter to the Romans in AD 57, he had never been to Rome. But by that time, Roman believers were meeting in house churches.

Paul wrote his letter in part to explain the essentials of the Christian faith and what it means to live for Jesus. Paul's words are helpful to Christians today. As you guide kids through Romans 5–6, help them grasp the good news of the gospel. This is the message for which Jesus' followers gave their lives. This good news changes everything.

First, help kids understand the benefits of believing in Jesus. To appreciate the good news, kids need to understand the bad news: Apart from Jesus, we are dead in our sin—separated from God. We need to be rescued. God sent Jesus into the world to rescue sinners. When we trust in His death and resurrection, we are made right with God and are saved from sin and death.

Next, compare and contrast the first Adam with Jesus—"the second Adam." Adam represented all people, but he sinned. Sin brought death into the world, and death spread to all people because all people sinned. Jesus came to bring us life. He obeyed God perfectly. All who trust in Him are forgiven and have eternal life.

Finally, introduce how believers deal with sin in view of God's grace. Since our sin is forgiven, should we keep on sinning? Paul was emphatic that the answer is no. When we are in Christ, we are no longer slaves to sin. Sin will still be a struggle in our fallen world, but we have power through the Holy Spirit to resist sin and live a life that honors God.

The BIBLE Story

The Good News
Romans 5–6

Jesus' followers in **the early church wanted everyone to hear the good news about Jesus. God** had kept His promise to send a Savior. He **sent His own Son, Jesus, to earth to rescue sinners. Jesus lived the perfect life** we cannot live **and died the death we deserve** to die. **On the third day, God raised Jesus from the dead!**

This good news—**the gospel—changes everything.** People who love Jesus tell others about Him. That's what Paul did. **Paul wrote a letter to believers in Rome** to tell them that Jesus was the Savior they had been waiting for.

Paul wrote, "I am not ashamed of the gospel, because it is the power of God for salvation to everyone who believes." Everyone sins and needs to be rescued. **God saves people who believe the good news about Jesus.** Because of their faith, God forgives their sins and gives them eternal life.

Paul wrote that God showed His love for us by sending His Son to die for us. "We were sinners— enemies of God—**but Jesus died and rose again to make us right with God.** Jesus is God's good gift to us. Let's rejoice!"

Paul reminded the people about the first man, **Adam. When**

Younger Kids Leader Guide
Unit 29 • Session 3

Adam sinned, death came into the world. Everyone sinned, so death spread to all people. God sent Jesus into the world to bring us a gift that is greater than Adam's sin. **Adam brought death, but Jesus brings life. Adam disobeyed God, but Jesus obeyed Him perfectly.**

Does that mean we can keep on sinning because we are forgiven? **Paul said no! Jesus sets us free from sin** so we can live in a new way that honors Him.

Christ Connection: Because God created everything, He is in charge of everything. Everyone sins, or disobeys God. Our sin separates us from God. The good news of the gospel is that God sent His Son, Jesus, to take the punishment we deserve. Everyone who trusts in Jesus will be saved.

Bible Storytelling Tips

• **Use music:** Incorporate atmospheric background music that fits with the story. Play triumphant music while speaking about Jesus' resurrection. Play sad music when talking about Adam and sin in the world.

INTRODUCE the Story

SESSION TITLE: The Good News

BIBLE PASSAGE: Romans 5–6

STORY POINT: God sent Jesus into the world to rescue sinners.

KEY PASSAGE: Romans 12:5

BIG PICTURE QUESTION: What is the church? The church is all Christians everywhere, who gather together in their communities to worship and serve God.

Welcome time

Greet each kid as he or she arrives. Use this time to collect the offering, fill out attendance sheets, and help new kids connect to your group. Prompt kids to tell about a time they got to share good news with someone else.

SAY • It feels good to tell someone happy news. Whether it's the announcement of a new baby's birth or telling your parents about the good grade you got, good news feels good to share. Today we will learn about a letter Paul wrote to explain the best news of all—the gospel—to believers in Rome.

Activity page (5 minutes)

- "All Fixed Up" activity page, 1 per kid
- pencils or markers

Invite kids to complete the "All Fixed Up" activity page. Kids must match each 2D shape with the 3D figure it would make if folded.

SAY • In each of those shapes, you could kind of see what it was supposed to look like when it was fixed up. In a way, that's like our story today. We will talk about the good news of the gospel, and how Jesus showed perfectly what Adam was supposed to be like before he chose to disobey God.

Session starter (10 minutes)

LOW PREP

OPTION 1: Telephone game

Instruct the kids to sit in a line. Whisper a secret message, such as the story point, into the first kid's ear. He will whisper it in the ear of the kid behind him, and so on down the line. Allow the last kid to say aloud what she heard. Play as time allows or until each kid has a chance to be the end of the line.

SAY • If you whisper a message and only say it once, it's easy to have the message become distorted. Today we will learn about a time Paul wrote down the good news of the gospel in a letter for the believers in Rome, so they would know for sure what the gospel is.

OPTION 2: Roads to Rome

Form two teams of kids. Give each team two sheets of paper. You may choose to use something more durable, like carpet squares, if you have them available. The teams will form two lines, and the first kid in each line will use the two sheets of paper as stepping stones to cross the room and return to the line. There they will pass their two sheets to the next kid in line who will repeat the process. The first team to have each member cross the room and return wins.

· sheets of paper, 4
· carpet squares, 4
 (optional)

SAY • In the time of the New Testament, Rome controlled a large empire that covered most of the known world. Because the Roman empire was so big and so powerful, they built many roads to help people travel around. That led to the saying "all roads lead to Rome." Today we will hear about a letter Paul wrote to believers living in Rome.

Transition to teach the story

The Early Church

TEACH the Story

SESSION TITLE: The Good News

BIBLE PASSAGE: Romans 5–6

STORY POINT: God sent Jesus into the world to rescue sinners.

KEY PASSAGE: Romans 12:5

BIG PICTURE QUESTION: What is the church? The church is all Christians everywhere, who gather together in their communities to worship and serve God.

Countdown

· countdown video

Show the countdown video as you transition to teach the story. Set it to end as the session begins.

Introduce the session (3 minutes)

· leader attire

[Leader enters wearing nice clothing and white gloves.]

LEADER • Hey friends. It's good to see you here again. For those of you who are new, my name is *[your name]* and I'm an expert coin collector. I teach this coin collecting seminar from my shop. My hope is that I can help anyone get interested in coins and begin their collection on the right foot with the knowledge they need.

Tip: If you prefer not to use themed content or characters, adapt or omit this introduction.

Any time you are teaching, it's important to walk people through the information in a step-by-step, easy-to-follow way. That's why my class always starts with a brief history of coins, then moves on to how coins are made today, and finally begins to discuss how to find valuable coins and what makes different coins valuable.

One thing that can make a coin valuable is a mistake on the coin. The machines used to make modern coins are very precise, so mistakes in the production don't happen often; mistakes that end up going out into circulation—well, those are more rare! It's important to know things like how a coin is made so you can know when a coin has an error.

In a way, this makes me think of our Bible story. Paul wanted to be sure that Roman believers knew the full gospel, so he explained the gospel in a very clear way. Like in coin collecting, knowing the truth of the gospel helps you spot errors. Knowing how God created the world to be helps you see that sin has broken it, and we need a Savior. Let's get to it.

Big picture question (1 minute)

LEADER • Jesus did not save us to live alone. He saved us to live alongside other believers as part of the church. *What is the church? The church is all Christians everywhere, who gather together in their communities to worship and serve God.* Believers meet together to encourage one another, teach each other about God, study God's Word, and live on mission to grow God's kingdom.

Giant timeline (1 minute)

Show the giant timeline. Point to individual Bible stories as you review.

· Giant Timeline

LEADER • Last week we learned about Stephen. **Stephen preached about Jesus no matter what.** When religious leaders killed Stephen because of his preaching, the believers living in Jerusalem began to leave and spread out to get away from persecution. As they spread out, they told more people about

Jesus, and the gospel reached further and further. Eventually it reached Rome. Paul, an apostle of God wrote a letter to the believers in Rome to make sure they understood the gospel. Our story today is called "The Good News."

Tell the Bible story (10 minutes)

Open your Bible to Romans 5–6. Use the Bible storytelling tips on the Bible story page to help you tell the story, or show the Bible story video "The Good News."

LEADER • Paul's comparison of Adam to Jesus is really important. Looking at Adam before and after he sinned helps us see both what God's creation is supposed to be like, and how sin has damaged God's good work.

Adam was supposed to choose obedience to God, but instead chose to rebel against God. Adam rejected God's authority and tried to become wise by eating the fruit of the knowledge of good and evil. His sinful choice brought pain, sadness, death, and destruction into the world.

Jesus, on the other hand, chose not to sin. He lived a perfect life. He showed us exactly what God is like by displaying God's power and glory. Jesus submitted to the Father's authority and, despite being God the Son, died on the cross—the death we deserve. His righteousness and sacrifice made the way for joy, peace, life, and restoration to come into the world through faith in Him.

Christ connection

LEADER • Because God created everything, He is in charge

- Bibles
- "The Good News" video
- Big Picture Question Poster
- Bible Story Picture Poster
- Story Point Poster

Note: You may use this opportunity to use Scripture and the guide provided to explain how to become a Christian. Make sure kids know when and where they can ask questions.

Younger Kids Leader Guide
Unit 29 • Session 3

of everything. Everyone sins, or disobeys God. Our sin separates us from God. The good news of the gospel is that God sent His Son, Jesus, to take the punishment we deserve. Everyone who trusts in Jesus will be saved.

Questions from kids video (3 minutes)

Show the "Unit 29, Session 3" questions from kids video. Prompt kids to think about when they first heard the gospel. Guide them to discuss why it's important for believers to tell others about Jesus.

· "Unit 29, Session 3" Questions from Kids video

Missions moment (3 minutes)

Play the "Starting Churches in Minneapolis" video, then ask kids to discuss how the church is reaching people from Africa with the good news.

· "Starting Churches in Minneapolis" missions video

LEADER • Church planters Philip and Jummai Nache have very good news to share with the people of Minneapolis, Minnesota. God provided Jesus to die for our sins and give us eternal life. As they share that gospel message with more people, and those people put their faith in Jesus, the church grows! *What is the church? The church is all Christians everywhere, who gather together in their communities to worship and serve God.*

Key passage (5 minutes)

Show the key passage poster. Lead the boys and girls to read together Romans 12:5. Then sing the key passage song.

· Key Passage Poster
· "We Who Are Many (Romans 12:5)" song

LEADER • In Paul's letter to the Romans, he also explained the nature of the church. Many individual people come together to make one body. And Jesus is the

The Early Church

head of that body. Because of Jesus, we can all have equal standing before God. We are all sinners and we can all be saved by grace through faith in Jesus.

Sing (4 minutes)

· "One Foundation" song

LEADER • Jesus is the rock on which the church is built. Let's sing praises to Him, the foundation we need. Sing together "One Foundation."

Pray (2 minutes)

Invite kids to pray before dismissing to apply the story.

LEADER • Father, thank You for sending Jesus. We are sinners and we desperately needed Your love to save us. We know that there is no one who can earn salvation. Thank You for giving it freely to everyone who has faith. Help us to live for Your glory. Amen.

Dismiss to apply the story

The Gospel: God's Plan for Me

Ask kids if they have ever heard the word *gospel*. Clarify that the word *gospel* means "good news." It is the message about Christ, the kingdom of God, and salvation. Use the following guide to share the gospel with kids.

God rules. Explain to kids that the Bible tells us God created everything, and He is in charge of everything. Invite a volunteer to read Genesis 1:1 from the Bible. Read Revelation 4:11 or Colossians 1:16-17 aloud and explain what these verses mean.

We sinned. Tell kids that since the time of Adam and Eve, everyone has chosen to disobey God. (Romans 3:23) The Bible calls this sin. Because God is holy, God cannot be around sin. Sin separates us from God and deserves God's punishment of death. (Romans 6:23)

God provided. Choose a child to read John 3:16 aloud. Say that God sent His Son, Jesus, the perfect solution to our sin problem, to rescue us from the punishment we deserve. It's something we, as sinners, could never earn on our own. Jesus alone saves us. Read and explain Ephesians 2:8-9.

Jesus gives. Share with kids that Jesus lived a perfect life, died on the cross for our sins, and rose again. Because Jesus gave up His life for us, we can be welcomed into God's family for eternity. This is the best gift ever! Read Romans 5:8; 2 Corinthians 5:21; or 1 Peter 3:18.

We respond. Tell kids that they can respond to Jesus. Read Romans 10:9-10,13. Review these aspects of our response: Believe in your heart that Jesus alone saves you through what He's already done on the cross. Repent, turning from self and sin to Jesus. Tell God and others that your faith is in Jesus.

Offer to talk with any child who is interested in responding to Jesus. Provide *I'm a Christian Now!* for new Christians to take home and complete with their families.

APPLY the Story

SESSION TITLE: The Good News

BIBLE PASSAGE: Romans 5–6

STORY POINT: God sent Jesus into the world to rescue sinners.

KEY PASSAGE: Romans 12:5

BIG PICTURE QUESTION: What is the church? The church is all Christians everywhere, who gather together in their communities to worship and serve God.

Key passage activity (5 minutes)

- Key Passage Poster
- Allergy Alert
- balloon

Inflate a balloon and tie it off. Challenge the kids to work together to keep the balloon in the air by bopping it one at a time. No kid may bop the balloon more than three times total, no kid may bop it more than once consecutively, and each kid must say a word of the key passage to bop the balloon. Each time the balloon hits the floor, stop the game and start it over.

SAY • Paul wrote these words as part of his letter to believer in Rome. That's the letter our story came from today! In addition to making sure they understood the gospel, Paul wanted them to know that believers form one body, united together by Jesus. That's still true for believers today!

Discussion & Bible skills (10 minutes)

- Bibles, 1 per kid
- Story Point Poster
- Small Group Timeline and Map Set (005802970, optional)

Distribute a Bible to each kid. Help kids find Romans 5–6. Explain that Romans is the first of Paul's Letters, a division in the New Testament containing letters Paul wrote to believers in cities all over the Roman Empire. In total, Paul wrote 13 of the 21 books of the New Testament! Point out Rome on the New Testament Mediterranean Map. (*B1*)

Ask the following questions. Lead the group to discuss:

Option: Retell or review the Bible story using the bolded text of the Bible story script.

1. How is a person justified—given a right relationship with God? (*by faith in Jesus' sacrifice, Romans 5:1, 9*)

2. Through whom did sin enter the world? (*Adam, Romans 5:12*)

3. Through whom does righteousness and justification come? (*Jesus, Romans 5:18-19*)

4. Does it feel fair or unfair that Adam's sin led to sin for all of us? *Guide kids to see that all of us have sin. We aren't guilty simply because of Adam's sin, but also because of our own sins. Help them see this truth through the lens of Christ's sacrifice making righteousness available to all despite our sin.*

5. Does it feel fair or unfair that Jesus' righteousness leads to righteousness for all who have faith? *Help kids see that this, too, is a picture of God's perfect justice. He showed us mercy when Christ became our perfect substitute. Help the kids wrestle with the difference between human ideas about justice and fairness in contrast to God's perfect justice and mercy.*

6. If God forgives all our sin when we have faith in Jesus, why is it necessary to live like Jesus? *Guide kids to remember that God's plan for our lives is better for us than our own plans. Obeying God is good for us, because He knows what we need before we need it. Help them see obedience as a blessing, not a chore. Explain how sin may feel fun, but it leads to destruction, pain, and death.*

SAY • **God sent Jesus into the world to rescue sinners**. The Bible is clear that we all are sinners and we all deserve death and separation from God. His choice to send Jesus proves His justice and mercy.

Activity choice (10 minutes)

OPTION 1: Carry the message home

Display a map of the US and a map of Africa. Ask volunteers to find some of the countries mentioned in the video such as Sudan, Nigeria, Ethiopia, and Cameroon.

Allow the kids to place pins in the Twin Cities, and each of the countries mentioned above. Then use string to connect the pins.

SAY • Churches give money to support the work of the Hope of Nations Gospel Church in Minnesota. But churches are really supporting missions around the world! Many of the immigrants who hear the good news eventually travel back to Africa, and they take the good news with them! How can we carry the good news with us?

OPTION 2: Read all about it

Provide kids with large sheets of paper, pencils, markers, and rulers. Invite the kids to design a newspaper front page based on the information in today's story. Encourage them to write a paragraph or two summarizing what they learned, or draw a large picture that represents what they learned.

SAY • Paul wrote to the believers in Rome to explain the gospel to them. Paul wanted to be sure they knew the truth and were following Jesus. He wanted them to know that **God sent Jesus into the world to rescue sinners**. Paul wanted them to experience the transformation that is only possible by the Holy Spirit's power and to be united together as a church body.

· US map
· world map
· string
· scissors
· push pins or tape

Tip: Use this activity option to reinforce the missions moment found in Teach the Story.

LOW PREP

· large sheets of paper
· pencils
· markers
· rulers

Reflection and prayer (5 minutes)

Distribute a sheet of paper to each child. Ask the kids to write about or draw a picture to answer the following questions:

- What does this story teach me about God or about the gospel?
- What does this story teach me about myself?
- Whom can I tell about this story?

Make sure to send the sheets home with kids alongside the activity page so that parents can see what their kids have been learning.

If time remains, take prayer requests or allow kids to complete the Bible story coloring page provided with this session. Pray for your group.

· pencils and crayons
· paper
· Bible Story Coloring Page, 1 per kid

Tip: Give parents this week's Big Picture Cards for Families to allow families to interact with the biblical content at home.

Unit 29 · Session 4
Doers of the Word

BIBLE PASSAGE:
James 1–2

STORY POINT:
James said that faith without works is useless.

KEY PASSAGE:
Romans 12:5

BIG PICTURE QUESTION:
What is the church? The church is all Christians everywhere, who gather together in their communities to worship and serve God.

INTRODUCE THE STORY
(10–15 MINUTES)
PAGE 140

→

TEACH THE STORY
(25–30 MINUTES)
PAGE 142

→

APPLY THE STORY
(25–30 MINUTES)
PAGE 148

Leaders, grow on the go! Listen to session-by-session training every week on Ministry Grid, Apple Podcasts, Spotify, or LifeWay's Digital Pass: ministrygrid.com/gospelproject | gospelproject.com/podcasts

LEADER Bible Study

The early church was made up mostly of Jewish believers who had grown up believing they needed to fully obey God to be accepted. Grace was a new concept for them, and many struggled with understanding how grace and obedience fit together. Some made the mistake of thinking that once they had acceptance in Jesus, obedience didn't matter after all.

This greatly concerned James—Jesus' half-brother and a leader in the church at Jerusalem— so he wrote a letter to the Jewish Christians scattered throughout the Roman Empire. James wanted these Christians to understand that grace and obedience do not work against each other; they work with each other.

James wrote, "Be doers of the word. If you hear the word but don't do it, you fool yourselves. Anyone who is a hearer but not a doer is like someone who looks at himself in a mirror, goes away and forgets right away what he looked like."

James wanted Christians to realize that true faith in Jesus—a faith that comes by grace—will always lead to action. True faith is an active faith.

James gave an example: When we look into a mirror and see something is not right—our hair is out of place or food is stuck in our teeth—we don't just walk away; we fix it. The gospel is like that mirror. It shows us what is true about ourselves, and when we see we are not living out our true identity, we should want to address it.

Help kids understand that true faith in Jesus always leads to living differently. When we trust in Jesus, God changes our hearts so that we will want to live a life pleasing to Him. We aren't accepted by God because of our obedience; we obey God out of gratitude because we are accepted by Him through Jesus.

The BIBLE Story

Doers of the Word
James 1–2

James was a leader in the Jerusalem church. He **wrote a letter to the Jewish believers** who had moved to many different places. **He told them the way believers should live.**

James explained that talking about God and the church is not enough. We have to do what God says. James wrote, "Be doers of the word. If you hear the word but don't do it, you fool yourselves. Anyone who is a hearer but not a doer is like someone who looks at himself in a mirror, goes away, and forgets right away what he looked like." **God's Word shows us the truth about ourselves. Anyone who hears and does the Word will be blessed.**

James explained that **people who really love God will show care to people too. God is honored when believers show their faith with actions. One way to do this is by helping orphans and widows**—people who are who have no one to take care of them.

We show love in what we say and do. James also wrote, "What good is it if someone says he has faith but does not do what is good and right? If someone is cold and hungry and you say to him, 'Go in peace, stay warm, and be well fed,' but you don't give

him clothes or food, what good is it?" James said that in the same way, faith without works is useless.

Anyone can say that he has faith, but true faith is proven by good works. James reminded the believers that **Abraham showed his faith when he obeyed God and got ready to sacrifice his son Isaac. Rahab showed her faith by risking her life to hide the spies in Jericho.**

God does not accept people because they do what is good and right; He accepts people who have true faith in Jesus. We can see that true faith when someone does what is good and right. **Faith comes first, and then doing what is good and right comes next.**

Christ Connection: Jesus said, "If anyone loves me, he will keep my word" (John 14:23). James reminded believers to be doers of the word. Jesus rescues us from sin and frees us to live a life that honors God. By doing what is good and right, people who trust Jesus can show that they really believe in Him.

Bible Storytelling Tips

- **Use props:** Bring props to help you tell the story. Reveal a mirror, play food, and warm clothing as you get to the pertinent parts of the story.
- **Go vertical:** Use a step ladder to add vertical movement to your storytelling technique. Stand higher on the ladder when discussing obedience to God, and stand lower when taking about those who say they have faith but do not bear fruit..

INTRODUCE the Story

SESSION TITLE: Doers of the Word

BIBLE PASSAGE: James 1–2

STORY POINT: James said that faith without works is useless.

KEY PASSAGE: Romans 12:5

BIG PICTURE QUESTION: What is the church? The church is all Christians everywhere, who gather together in their communities to worship and serve God.

Welcome time

Greet each kid as he or she arrives. Use this time to collect the offering, fill out attendance sheets, and help new kids connect to your group. Prompt kids to discuss the rules they have at their schools or in their homes. Is it important just to know the rules, or is it important to follow them as well?

SAY • Your teachers and parents give you rules for good reasons, to keep you safe and help you learn. To honor your teachers and parents, and to get the benefit of the rules, you need to do more than just know what the rules are. You need to follow them! God gives us rules for good reasons, too, and it's important to know them and follow them!

Activity page (5 minutes)

- "Finders of the Words" activity page, 1 per kid
- pencils or markers

Invite kids to complete the "Finders of the Words" activity page. Kids will use the key to find the words hidden in the grid of letters.

SAY • In that activity, you had to do more than just know the words that were hidden, you had to find them! Today we will learn about a time James told people to do more than just hear God's Word.

Younger Kids Leader Guide
Unit 29 • Session 4

Session starter (10 minutes)

OPTION 1: Ships and sailors

Instruct kids that they will play a game where they have to listen carefully for directions in order to know what to do. Instruct them to run to one side of the room when the leader says "ships," and to the other side when the leader says "sailors." When the leader says "captain's coming," kids will stand at attention and salute. When the leader says "three sailors rowing," three kids get in a line and pretend to row. Any child that takes too long to follow the command or cannot find the right number of partners is asked to sit out until the next round of play.

SAY • You had to listen carefully to know what to do and do it quickly to avoid being "out." It was important to both hear my words and do them. In today's Bible story, we'll hear about how important it is to both hear and do the Word of the Lord.

OPTION 2: Chopstick relay

Instruct kids to get into two lines. Each team should have a pair of chopsticks and a bowl of pom-poms. Place two empty bowls at the other end of the room. Show kids how to hold chopsticks and pick up the pom-poms. Kids will compete to move the pom-poms from one bowl to the other using only the chopsticks. If kids drop a pom-pom, they can pick it up with chopsticks and keep going. The first team to get all pom-poms to the other bowl wins.

SAY • It was important to use both chopsticks to pick up the pom-poms. Today, we will learn that two things are needed to follow Jesus: both faith and works!

Transition to teach the story

LOW PREP

Tip: You can search online for additional commands and actions to go with them.

· chopsticks, 2 pairs
· bowls, 4
· pom-poms

TEACH the Story

SESSION TITLE: Doers of the Word
BIBLE PASSAGE: James 1–2
STORY POINT: James said that faith without works is useless.
KEY PASSAGE: Romans 12:5
BIG PICTURE QUESTION: What is the church? The church is all Christians everywhere, who gather together in their communities to worship and serve God.

Countdown

· countdown video

Show the countdown video as you transition to teach the story. Set it to end as the session begins.

Introduce the session (3 minutes)

· leader attire

[Leader enters wearing nice clothing and white gloves.]

Tip: If you prefer not to use themed content or characters, adapt or omit this introduction.

LEADER • Hey everyone. Welcome to my shop. I'm glad you could make it back for the class. I had the strangest experience yesterday. I got an email from a man who described himself as the greatest coin collector of the 21st century. Naturally, I was excited to meet him and see his coins, so I emailed him back and we scheduled a time for me to go and see his collection.

Imagine how disappointed I was when I arrived and found out that all he had in his "collection" was a bunch of catalogs of coin values. He spoke a lot about how valuable this, that, or the other coin is, but he didn't actually own any of the coins he had read about in his collector's guides. Now, I'm not trying to tell people how to enjoy their hobby. If reading about coins is how he wants to enjoy coins,

I can't really tell him he's wrong ... but I also think it seems kind of silly to say he's a coin collector when he hasn't collected any coins.

You know, that reminds me of our Bible story. Do you think that a person can say they are a Christian if they don't really obey Christ? James wrote a letter that helps us understand why the church must obey Jesus' commands.

Big picture question (1 minute)

LEADER • We have been learning about the church. Namely, *what is the church? The church is all believers everywhere, who gather in their communities to worship and serve God.* There are many ways to worship God and many ways to serve Him. When we obey His commands, we can show with our actions that we believe in Jesus and that His love fills us up. Many of Jesus' commands have to do with taking care of other people and loving them well.

Giant timeline (1 minute)

Show the giant timeline. Point to individual Bible stories as you review.

· Giant Timeline

LEADER • At this point in the big story, Jesus had already come to earth, died on the cross for our sins in our place, and rose again showing His victory over sin and death for us. Jesus sent out the apostles to share the good news about Him and to start His church. As the good news spread, churches started everywhere, and leaders like James wrote letters to help these churches know how to honor God. Our story today is called "Doers of the Word."

The Early Church

Tell the Bible story (10 minutes)

- Bibles
- "Doers of the Word" video
- Big Picture Question Poster
- Bible Story Picture Poster
- Story Point Poster

Open your Bible to James 1–2. Use the Bible storytelling tips on the Bible story page to help you tell the story, or show the Bible story video "Doers of the Word."

LEADER • I love how simply James explained the importance of knowing God and obeying Him. If you were hungry, and someone told you that they hoped you were full, that wouldn't make you full, would it? No! They would need to actually feed you something to make you full. The same goes for if you are cold. Saying "Stay warm," may be a kind gesture, but it won't keep you from getting frostbite in cold weather. When you say one thing and your actions don't match up, it communicates to other people that you did not mean what you said.

We can't truly help others or please God by just knowing what God says to do. We must actually do it. Obeying God shows the world that we really are God's people, and Jesus really is our King. More than that, obedience is one way we show that we love God for all He has done for us. The church must love God and people. *What is the church? The church is all believers everywhere, who gather in their communities to worship and serve God.*

God loved us so much that He sent Jesus to die for us. We love Him in return by trusting that what He asks us to do is right and good for us, and then doing it! Just like Abraham showed that he believed God by being willing to sacrifice Isaac, we show that we love and trust God by believing His commands are good for us and others, and obeying Him. We can't just have faith, we must obey God and do the works He asks us to do. **James said that faith without works is useless.**

Christy connection

LEADER • Jesus said, "If anyone loves Me, he will keep My word" (John 14:23). James reminded believers to be doers of the word. Jesus rescues us from sin and frees us to live a life that honors God. By doing what is good and right, people who trust Jesus can show that they really believe in Him.

Note: You may use this opportunity to use Scripture and the guide provided to explain how to become a Christian. Make sure kids know when and where they can ask questions.

Questions from kids video (3 minutes)

Show the "Unit 29, Session 4" questions from kids video. Prompt kids to think about the reason we do good deeds. Guide them to discuss what our good deeds communicate to others.

· "Unit 29, Session 4" Questions from Kids video

Missions moment (3 minutes)

Read the story from the "Not a Lost Boy Anymore" printable. You may select a strong reader to read the story for the group.

· "Not a Lost Boy Anymore" printable

LEADER • People like Philip and Jummai Nache are showing through their words and actions that Jesus is the most important thing in their lives. They are willing to live for Him. The story of James from Africa helps us understand the importance of doing what the Bible says. In the Bible, **James said that faith without works is useless.**

Key passage (5 minutes)

Show the key passage poster. Lead the boys and girls to read together Romans 12:5. Then sing the key passage song.

· Key Passage Poster
· "We Who Are Many (Romans 12:5)" song

LEADER • Paul wrote this key passage as part of his letter to believers living in Rome. He wanted Christians to understand that we are all united as members of the church, the same way arms, legs, lungs, and so forth are united as parts of a body. Jesus is the head of the church. He's the ultimate authority. If you do not listen to and obey Him, you are like a body part that won't perform its job when your brain tells it to. That's not a good way to live.

Sing (4 minutes)

• "One Foundation" song

LEADER • Christ is both the head of the church body, and the foundation on which the church is built. Without Him, there is no church! That's why we worship Him.

Sing together "One Foundation."

Pray (2 minutes)

Invite kids to pray before dismissing to apply the story.

LEADER • God, thank You that You love us so much that You sent Jesus to die for us. Since we know that You did that for us, we know that You want good for us and that all Your commands are for our good. Help us to show our love for You by obeying You, showing that our faith is real by the works that we do. Amen.

Dismiss to apply the story

The Gospel: God's Plan for Me

Ask kids if they have ever heard the word *gospel*. Clarify that the word *gospel* means "good news." It is the message about Christ, the kingdom of God, and salvation. Use the following guide to share the gospel with kids.

God rules. Explain to kids that the Bible tells us God created everything, and He is in charge of everything. Invite a volunteer to read Genesis 1:1 from the Bible. Read Revelation 4:11 or Colossians 1:16-17 aloud and explain what these verses mean.

We sinned. Tell kids that since the time of Adam and Eve, everyone has chosen to disobey God. (Romans 3:23) The Bible calls this sin. Because God is holy, God cannot be around sin. Sin separates us from God and deserves God's punishment of death. (Romans 6:23)

God provided. Choose a child to read John 3:16 aloud. Say that God sent His Son, Jesus, the perfect solution to our sin problem, to rescue us from the punishment we deserve. It's something we, as sinners, could never earn on our own. Jesus alone saves us. Read and explain Ephesians 2:8-9.

Jesus gives. Share with kids that Jesus lived a perfect life, died on the cross for our sins, and rose again. Because Jesus gave up His life for us, we can be welcomed into God's family for eternity. This is the best gift ever! Read Romans 5:8; 2 Corinthians 5:21; or 1 Peter 3:18.

We respond. Tell kids that they can respond to Jesus. Read Romans 10:9-10,13. Review these aspects of our response: Believe in your heart that Jesus alone saves you through what He's already done on the cross. Repent, turning from self and sin to Jesus. Tell God and others that your faith is in Jesus.

Offer to talk with any child who is interested in responding to Jesus. Provide *I'm a Christian Now!* for new Christians to take home and complete with their families.

APPLY the Story

SESSION TITLE: Doers of the Word

BIBLE PASSAGE: James 1–2

STORY POINT: James said that faith without works is useless.

KEY PASSAGE: Romans 12:5

BIG PICTURE QUESTION: What is the church? The church is all Christians everywhere, who gather together in their communities to worship and serve God.

Key passage activity (5 minutes)

- Key Passage Poster
- index cards
- pens
- stopwatch (optional)

Prior to the session, write two to three words from the key passage on index cards. Give one card to each child, and then instruct the children to race to get in the right order. Mix up the cards again and see if kids can beat their time. Continue to practice the key passage in this way as long as kids are interested.

SAY • Paul wrote this key passage in his letter to the believers in Rome. Paul hadn't met them, but he wanted to be sure they knew the gospel and were united by God's grace.

Today, God's grace still unites believers. Everyone who is a Christian is a part of the global church, and we meet together in our communities to form local churches. When we love God, we obey His Word by serving and worshiping together.

Discussion & Bible skills (10 minutes)

- Bibles, 1 per kid
- Story Point Poster
- Small Group Timeline and Map Set (005802970, optional)

Distribute a Bible to each kid. Help them find James 1–2. Remind them that James is in the General Letters division of the New Testament, after Hebrews and before 1 Peter. James, Jesus' half-brother, wrote this book.

Ask the following questions. Lead the group to discuss:

1. James says that a person who hears the Word of God but does not do what it says is like who? (*A person who sees himself in a mirror and then immediately forgets what he looks like, James 1:23-24*)

2. What two groups of people did James specifically mention helping? (*widows and orphans, James 1:27*)

3. What does James say a person can show their faith by? (*the works they do to obey God, James 2:18*)

4. If you take care of people in need and show kindness to others, but do not trust Jesus, are you saved? *Remind kids that faith is necessary to salvation. We cannot earn salvation by good works.*

5. Why is faith without works useless? *Guide kids to understand that a person who claims faith but shows no outward signs of loving and obeying God's Word probably does not have true faith. Explain that saving faith is marked by the Holy Spirit's presence in a person's life. He transforms people to live more and more like Jesus; a person who isn't being transformed likely doesn't have the Holy Spirit in his life.*

6. What are some ways we can do good works through faith? *Help kids brainstorm practical ways they can live on mission, such as sharing their lunch with a friend, showing kindness to someone they don't normally get along with, and telling their friends about Jesus.*

Option: Retell or review the Bible story using the bolded text of the Bible story script.

SAY • James' letter was written mostly to Jewish believers. He wanted them to be prepared for hard times, and he wanted them to honor God with their actions, not just their words. **James said faith without works is useless.** We know that the Holy Spirit helps us do good works for God's glory.

The Early Church

· "Who to Tell"
  printable
· dry erase board or
  chalkboard
· dry erase marker or
  chalk
· tape

Tip: Use this
activity option
to reinforce the
missions moment
found in Teach the
Story.

**LOW
PREP**

· paper
· pencils
· scissors

Activity choice (10 minutes)

OPTION 1: Tell the world

Print and cut apart the "Who to Tell" printable.
Mix up the cards and distribute them face down among
the kids. On a dry erase board or chalkboard, make three
columns, labeled *Family*, *Friends*, and *Strangers*. Invite the
kids to reveal their cards and help them determine which
group each card fits into. Allow the kids to tape their cards
in place.

SAY • People took the time to tell James, the Lost Boy,
about Jesus. Church planters like Philip and Jummai
Nache are telling Africans that move to the U.S.
about Jesus. Who will you tell about Jesus?
        When we obey Jesus' command to tell others about
Him, we prove that we love Him. **James said that
faith without works is useless.** When we have faith,
the Holy Spirit helps us do the good things God has
prepared for us.

OPTION 2: Faith and works paper planes

Instruct kids to create paper airplanes, and write the word
FAITH on one wing, and *WORKS* on the other. Help kids
who may still be learning to write. Invite kids to line up and
see whose airplane will fly the farthest. Then, instruct kids
to cut off one wing of the airplane, whichever wing they
choose. Then invite the kids to compete again.

SAY • These airplanes sure flew a lot farther with both
wings, didn't they? Airplanes need both wings to
fly. In the same way, Christians need both faith and
works to please God. You can't have an airplane
without two wings, and you can't have true faith
without also obeying God and having good works.

Good works cannot save us, but **James said faith without works is useless.**

Reflection and prayer (5 minutes)

Distribute a sheet of paper to each child. Ask the kids to write about or draw a picture to answer the following questions:

- What does this story teach me about God or about the gospel?
- What does this story teach me about myself?
- Whom can I tell about this story?

Make sure to send the sheets home with kids alongside the activity page so that parents can see what their kids have been learning.

If time remains, take prayer requests or allow kids to complete the Bible story coloring page provided with this session. Pray for your group.

- pencils and crayons
- paper
- Bible Story Coloring Page, 1 per kid

Tip: Give parents this week's Big Picture Cards for Families to allow families to interact with the biblical content at home.

Unit 30: The Church Grew

Unit Description:

The early church's rapid growth led to some disagreements and problems. The leaders of the church addressed these problems by reminding everyone that Jesus is their ultimate leader and that they share the common mission given by Him to take the gospel to the entire world.

Key Passage:

Colossians 1:18

Big Picture Question:

Why does the church exist? The church exists to glorify God by worshiping Him, showing His love, and telling others about Jesus.

Session 1:

Philip and the Ethiopian
Acts 8

Story Point: The Holy Spirit led Philip to tell the Ethiopian man about Jesus.

Session 2:

Paul Met Jesus
Acts 8–9

Story Point: Jesus saved Paul and chose him to spread the gospel.

Session 3:

New Life in Jesus
Colossians 2–3

Story Point: Jesus gives new life to people who trust in Him.

Session 4:

Guarding the Truth
2 Corinthians 11

Story Point: God gives us power to stand up for the gospel.

Younger Kids Leader Guide

Philip and the Ethiopian

The Holy Spirit led Philip to tell the Ethiopian man about Jesus.

Paul Met Jesus

Jesus saved Paul and chose him to spread the gospel.

New Life in Jesus

Jesus gives new life to people who trust in Him.

Guarding the Truth

God gives us power to stand up for the gospel.

Unit 30 · Session 1
Philip and the Ethiopian

BIBLE PASSAGE:
Acts 8

STORY POINT:
The Holy Spirit led Philip to tell the Ethiopian man about Jesus.

KEY PASSAGE:
Colossians 1:18

BIG PICTURE QUESTION:
Why does the church exist? The church exists to glorify God by worshiping Him, showing His love, and telling others about Jesus.

INTRODUCE THE STORY (10–15 MINUTES) PAGE 158		TEACH THE STORY (25–30 MINUTES) PAGE 160		APPLY THE STORY (25–30 MINUTES) PAGE 166

Leaders, grow on the go! Listen to session-by-session training every week on Ministry Grid, Apple Podcasts, Spotify, or LifeWay's Digital Pass: ministrygrid.com/gospelproject | gospelproject.com/podcasts

LEADER Bible Study

The believers in the early church faced intense persecution. After Stephen was killed, Jesus' followers at the church in Jerusalem scattered; however, they did not stop talking about Jesus. They continued to share the good news. One man, Philip, took the gospel to Samaria. The crowds there listened and believed, and they had great joy.

In today's Bible story, Philip was instructed by an angel of the Lord to go to a certain road in the desert. Philip obeyed. The Spirit led Philip to a chariot, where an Ethiopian official was reading the Scriptures from the prophet Isaiah. The Ethiopian man did not understand what he was reading, so Philip explained it to him.

The man was reading from the prophet Isaiah: "He was led like a sheep to the slaughter ... In his humiliation justice was denied him ... For his life is taken from the earth" (Acts 8:32-33). The official wondered if Isaiah was speaking about himself or another person. Philip told the official that Isaiah's words weren't about Isaiah; they were about the Messiah—Jesus! The official believed in Jesus and was baptized.

Guide kids to consider the role of the Holy Spirit in this interaction between Philip and the Ethiopian official. Who was responsible for Philip's going to the desert? Who helped Philip explain the Scriptures? Who changed the heart of the official so he would believe?

After his interaction with the Ethiopian official, Philip continued sharing the gospel in all the towns on his way to the town of Caesarea.

In our mission of making disciples, believers must be willing instruments to be used in the hands of the Lord. Philip didn't go into the desert today with a strategy for converting another man; the Holy Spirit led Philip, and he obeyed. As believers, we can be open to the guidance of the Holy Spirit and willing to follow His lead. He will go with us.

The Church Grew

The **BIBLE** Story

Philip and the Ethiopian

Acts 8

An angel of the Lord told Philip, a follower of Jesus, **to go to a desert road** between Jerusalem and Gaza. So **Philip went.**

On the road was a man from Ethiopia. He was **an important official to the queen of Ethiopia**. The man had come to worship in Jerusalem, and now he was on his way home. **He sat in his chariot, reading aloud the words of the prophet Isaiah.**

The Holy Spirit told Philip to go to the chariot, so Philip ran up to it. **"Do you understand what you are reading?" Philip asked the man.**

The official replied, "How can I, unless someone explains it to me?" He invited Philip into his chariot, and Philip sat with him. **The official was reading these words from Isaiah:**

He was led like a sheep to the slaughter, and as a lamb is silent before its shearer, so He does not open His mouth. He was treated unfairly, and His life is taken away.

The official asked, "Was Isaiah talking about himself or someone else?" **Isaiah was talking about the Messiah, so Philip begin to tell the man the good news about Jesus.**

As they traveled down the road, **they came to some water. "What would keep me from being baptized?" the official asked.**

Then the official told the chariot to stop. **He and Philip went down into the water, and Philip baptized him. When they came up out of the water, the Holy Spirit took Philip away.** The official continued home, and he was very happy.

Christ Connection: The Ethiopian official knew what the Old Testament prophets said, but he did not understand that they spoke about Jesus. The Holy Spirit led Philip to help the official understand the good news about Jesus: Jesus died on the cross for our sins and was raised from the dead, just like the Old Testament prophets said.

Bible Storytelling Tips

- **Act it out:** Invite kid volunteers to act out the story as you tell it.
- **Call and Response:** Instruct the kids to listen for certain words or names, and respond in unison. For example, when you say Philip, they'll say "obeyed," when you say Ethiopian they'll say "believed," and when you say "Isaiah, they'll say "the prophet."

The Church Grew

INTRODUCE the Story

SESSION TITLE: Philip and the Ethiopian

BIBLE PASSAGE: Acts 8

STORY POINT: The Holy Spirit led Philip to tell the Ethiopian man about Jesus.

KEY PASSAGE: Colossians 1:18

BIG PICTURE QUESTION: Why does the church exist? The church exists to glorify God by worshiping Him, showing His love, and telling others about Jesus.

Welcome time

Greet each kid as he or she arrives. Use this time to collect the offering, fill out attendance sheets, and help new kids connect to your group. Prompt kids to share about a time they made a new friend.

SAY • Meeting new friends is a great experience. If you meet someone who doesn't know Jesus, sharing the gospel with them is a great way to show them you care about them. Today we will learn about a man named Philip, who went to meet a new friend and help that friend understand the gospel.

Activity page (5 minutes)

· "The Desert Road" activity page, 1 per kid
· pencils or markers

Invite kids to complete the "The Desert Road" activity page. Ask the kids to solve the maze to help Philip reach the Ethiopian official.

SAY • Good job solving that maze. Today we will learn about a time Philip went to tell a man about Jesus. He didn't have to walk through a maze, but he was guided to the man! The Holy Spirit led Philip. We'll talk more about that later.

Session starter (10 minutes)

OPTION 1: Human chariot race

Form groups of three kids. Instruct each group to select two kids to be "horses" and one to be the "driver." The driver will stand slightly behind the two "horses" and place each hand on a shoulder of each kid. Each group will race to the far end of the room and back without breaking formation. The first group to complete three laps (down and back) wins.

SAY • A chariot is a special cart pulled by a horse or two. In Bible times, they were a quick way to get around, but usually only very important people had them. Today we will learn about a time the Holy Spirit sent Philip to a man riding in a chariot. Who do you think it could have been?

OPTION 2: Follow the leader

Select one kid to be the leader. She will walk around the room making noises and gestures. The other kids will follow behind her in a single file line mimicking all her actions. Every minute or so, rotate to a new leader.

SAY • Follow the leader is fun, and usually pretty easy to play. We will learn today about a time Philip followed the Holy Spirit's lead. Do you think what he had to do was easy? We'll learn more about it soon.

Transition to teach the story

TEACH the Story

SESSION TITLE: Philip and the Ethiopian

BIBLE PASSAGE: Acts 8

STORY POINT: The Holy Spirit led Philip to tell the Ethiopian man about Jesus.

KEY PASSAGE: Colossians 1:18

BIG PICTURE QUESTION: Why does the church exist? The church exists to glorify God by worshiping Him, showing His love, and telling others about Jesus.

· room decorations
· Theme Background Slide (optional)

Suggested Theme Decorating Ideas: Decorate the room to look like a soccer practice field. Use PVC pipes and netted fabric to simulate a soccer goal. Place orange training cones to one side of the stage, and fill a mesh laundry bag with soccer balls to place at the other end of the area.

Countdown

· countdown video

Show the countdown video as you transition to teach the story. Set it to end as the session begins.

Introduce the session (3 minutes)

· leader attire

[Leader enters wearing khaki shorts and a polo shirt, with a whistle hanging from a lanyard around her neck.]

Tip: If you prefer not to use themed content or characters, adapt or omit this introduction.

LEADER • Hey everyone, welcome to the field. I'm glad you could all show up for the soccer team try-outs. We lost a lot of players last year when they aged out of our league, so we have tons of openings for great new players to step in.

You know, when I think about it, there's a lot of similarity between a soccer team and a church. Especially when we are recruiting new players. Both a soccer team and a church have to work together well. The members of both have to be willing to listen to their leaders to make sure their job is done well. But one major difference is that a soccer team only has a certain number of slots to fill before they stop recruiting players; Jesus' family is never full, and there's always room for more people who repent and believe the gospel to join the church. That makes me think of a cool story about one man who listened to the Holy Spirit to "recruit" a new believer. Let me tell you all about it.

Big picture question (1 minute)

LEADER • As we get into these new Bible stories, I want to get you thinking about a new big picture question. ***Why does the church exist?*** Remember that the church isn't a building, it's the people; believers who gather to glorify God. But why? Why does God unite believers into the church? Let's think on that question. I'll give you the answer after we hear the story.

Giant timeline (1 minute)

Show the giant timeline. Point to individual Bible stories as you review.   · Giant Timeline

LEADER • The early church definitely had some struggles. Some members were selfish, like Ananias and Sapphira. Other members were arrested, mistreated, hurt, or even killed because of their faith. But through it all, God was using the struggles to strengthen and grow the church in various ways. All of this was done by the Holy Spirit's power. Today, we will learn about a time one man led another to Jesus. Our story is called "Philip and the Ethiopian."

The Church Grew

Tell the Bible story (10 minutes)

- Bibles
- "Philip and the Ethiopian" video
- Big Picture Question Poster
- Bible Story Picture Poster
- Story Point Poster

Open your Bible to Acts 8. Use the Bible storytelling tips on the Bible story page to help you tell the story, or show the Bible story video "Philip and the Ethiopian."

LEADER • Sometimes I wish that every opportunity to share the gospel was as easy as walking up to a person and them asking me to help them understand the Bible. The Holy Spirit really set up an incredible situation for Philip. And because Philip obeyed joyfully, the Ethiopian official became a believer!

This story has a lot to teach us about immediate obedience. Philip didn't make excuses about how far away the desert road was, or how uncomfortable he would feel running up to a stranger's chariot to talk. Instead, he just obeyed. Jesus' final command to His disciples was to make disciples and baptize them. The early church took that command very seriously!

As soon as the Ethiopian man believed, he asked to be baptized to show his new faith. His obedience was immediate too. When Philip was carried away by the Spirit, the Ethiopian went on his way rejoicing. He was headed home, so we can know that he carried the truth of Jesus with him to Ethiopia! All along God's plan has been to glorify His name through the church. So, *why does the church exist? The church exists to glorify God by worshiping Him, showing His love, and telling others about Jesus.*

Christ connection

Note: You may use this opportunity to use Scripture and the guide provided to explain how to become a Christian. Make sure kids know when and where they can ask questions.

LEADER • The Ethiopian official knew what the Old Testament prophets said, but he did not understand that they spoke about Jesus. The Holy Spirit led

Philip to help the official understand the good news about Jesus: Jesus died on the cross for our sins and was raised from the dead, just like the Old Testament prophets said.

Questions from kids video (3 minutes)

Show the "Unit 30, Session 1" questions from kids video. Prompt kids to think about why it's good to have some friends who don't know Jesus. Guide them to discuss ways they could share the gospel with the lost.

· "Unit 30, Session 1" Questions from Kids video

Missions moment (3 minutes)

Play the "Together" missions video.

LEADER • The Holy Spirit tells people today to go and tell people about Jesus, like He told Philip to tell the Ethiopian man about Jesus. When Christians work together to share the gospel, we can reach more people all over the world.

Pray for missionaries all over the world, specifically any missionaries your church supports.

· "Together" missions video

Key passage (5 minutes)

Show the key passage poster. Lead the boys and girls to read together Colossians 1:18. Then sing the key passage song.

LEADER • Paul wrote this as part of his letter to believers in a city called Colossae. Paul wanted them to be sure they gave Jesus the respect and glory He deserves. He is our greatest treasure, and we exist as a church to tell people about Him.

· Key Passage Poster
· "First Place in Everything (Colossians 1:18)" song

Sing (4 minutes)

LEADER • Let's worship God and ask Him to help us live on

· "This Is Where the Mission Begins" song

mission together.

Sing together "This Is Where the Mission Begins."

Pray (2 minutes)

Invite kids to pray before dismissing to apply the story.

LEADER • Father, help us to love You most and obey You with joy. Give us courage to share the gospel boldly with everyone we meet. Amen.

Dismiss to apply the story

The Gospel: God's Plan for Me

Ask kids if they have ever heard the word *gospel*. Clarify that the word *gospel* means "good news." It is the message about Christ, the kingdom of God, and salvation. Use the following guide to share the gospel with kids.

God rules. Explain to kids that the Bible tells us God created everything, and He is in charge of everything. Invite a volunteer to read Genesis 1:1 from the Bible. Read Revelation 4:11 or Colossians 1:16-17 aloud and explain what these verses mean.

We sinned. Tell kids that since the time of Adam and Eve, everyone has chosen to disobey God. (Romans 3:23) The Bible calls this sin. Because God is holy, God cannot be around sin. Sin separates us from God and deserves God's punishment of death. (Romans 6:23)

God provided. Choose a child to read John 3:16 aloud. Say that God sent His Son, Jesus, the perfect solution to our sin problem, to rescue us from the punishment we deserve. It's something we, as sinners, could never earn on our own. Jesus alone saves us. Read and explain Ephesians 2:8-9.

Jesus gives. Share with kids that Jesus lived a perfect life, died on the cross for our sins, and rose again. Because Jesus gave up His life for us, we can be welcomed into God's family for eternity. This is the best gift ever! Read Romans 5:8; 2 Corinthians 5:21; or 1 Peter 3:18.

We respond. Tell kids that they can respond to Jesus. Read Romans 10:9-10,13. Review these aspects of our response: Believe in your heart that Jesus alone saves you through what He's already done on the cross. Repent, turning from self and sin to Jesus. Tell God and others that your faith is in Jesus.

Offer to talk with any child who is interested in responding to Jesus. Provide *I'm a Christian Now!* for new Christians to take home and complete with their families.

The Church Grew

APPLY the Story

SESSION TITLE: Philip and the Ethiopian

BIBLE PASSAGE: Acts 8

STORY POINT: The Holy Spirit led Philip to tell the Ethiopian man about Jesus.

KEY PASSAGE: Colossians 1:18

BIG PICTURE QUESTION: Why does the church exist? The church exists to glorify God by worshiping Him, showing His love, and telling others about Jesus.

Key passage activity (5 minutes)

· Key Passage Poster

Say the key passage together as a group multiple times, using different voices each time. Use the suggested voices below or come up with your own.

Suggested voices: high-pitched mouse voice, low-pitched giant voice, pirate voice, robot voice, and so forth.

SAY • Paul often talked about the church as the body. Jesus is the head of the church body! That means He is the most important. He leads and guides us. He is the greatest treasure, and the reason we can be saved. *Why does the church exist? The church exists to glorify God by worshiping Him, showing His love, and telling others about Jesus.*

Discussion & Bible skills (10 minutes)

· Bibles, 1 per kid
· Story Point Poster
· Small Group Timeline and Map Set (005802970, optional)

Distribute a Bible to each kid. Help them find Acts 8. Discuss which division of the Bible Acts is a part of. (*New Testament History*) Explain that Luke wrote the Book of Acts, and it serves almost as a sequel to the Gospel of Luke. Consider using the New Testament Israel Map to point out Jerusalem and Gaza. (*H5, I2*) Remind kids that Philip met the Ethiopian man on a road between the two places.

Ask the following questions. Lead the group to discuss:

Option: Retell or review the Bible story using the bolded text of the Bible story script.

1. Why did Philip travel to the spot where he met the Ethiopian official? (*The Holy Spirit told him to, Acts 8:26*)

2. Which prophet's writings was the Ethiopian official reading (*Isaiah's, Acts 8:30*)

3. How did the Ethiopian react to the gospel? (*he believed it and was baptized, Acts 8:36-39*)

4. How can we share the gospel with others? *Guide kids to think about the importance of being prepared to speak about God. Stress the importance of studying God's Word and praying for God to give us opportunities to share. Remind them that the Holy Spirit will guide us and give us wisdom to know what to say. Encourage them to look for ways to speak about the gospel in their everyday lives.*

5. What should we do if someone rejects the gospel? *Help the kids think about how to deal with rejection. Remind them that anyone who rejects the gospel is rejecting God, not us. We should be respectful and kind towards everyone, even those who reject the gospel. God doesn't want us to be discouraged by rejection, but encouraged by His power so that we continue sharing.*

6. Other than sharing the gospel, how can we show God's love to others? *Guide kids to think practically. They could help a classmate with homework, sit with someone new at lunch, share a cool toy with a sibling, or volunteer with their families to serve in a shelter or food bank. Help them see that there are many ways to show love, and all of them can lead to sharing the gospel.*

SAY • **The Holy Spirit led Philip to tell the Ethiopian man about Jesus.** We can share about Jesus too!

The Church Grew

Activity choice (10 minutes)

OPTION 1: Bedsheet bounce

Select a volunteer to compete against the rest of the group. Give both him and all the other kids a flat bedsheet and a playground ball. Challenge the team and the individual to use the bedsheet to toss and catch the ball. The group will spread out around the perimeter of the sheet and hold it taut, using the sheet as a parachute to toss the ball up and catch it. The individual will be unable to manage the task. After a minute or so, allow all the kids to work together to continue tossing the ball.

Tip: Use this activity option to reinforce the missions moment found in Teach the Story.

SAY • That game was much better with friends to help you; playing alone was much harder. That's a little like the Christian life. We all need one another.

Missions is often about working together to do what God has commanded us to do. Churches all over the country give money, pray, and work together to send missionaries to all nations. It's better when we work together!

OPTION 2: Jesus is the lamb

· paper plates, 1 per kid
· cotton balls
· glue sticks

Provide a paper plate and four craft sticks to each kid. Provide the kids with cotton balls and glue sticks. Help the kids draw a face on the plate and glue cotton around the edges so that it looks like a fluffy lamb. On the back of the plate, help the kids write the Story Point and the reference Isaiah 53:7.

SAY • **The Holy Spirit led Philip to tell the Ethiopian man about Jesus.** The Ethiopian was reading from Isaiah, and he did not understand who was like a lamb let to be slaughtered. Philip explained that Isaiah was writing about Jesus, and then he told the man about Jesus' death and resurrection. The man believed and was baptized. We can share the gospel just like Philip did, and we can even use our paper plate lambs to help us talk about Jesus.

Reflection and prayer (5 minutes)

Distribute a sheet of paper to each child. Ask the kids to write about or draw a picture to answer the following questions:

- What does this story teach me about God or about the gospel?
- What does this story teach me about myself?
- Whom can I tell about this story?

Make sure to send the sheets home with kids alongside the activity page so that parents can see what their kids have been learning.

If time remains, take prayer requests or allow kids to complete the Bible story coloring page provided with this session. Pray for your group.

· pencils and crayons
· paper
· Bible Story Coloring Page, 1 per kid

Tip: Give parents this week's Big Picture Cards for Families to allow families to interact with the biblical content at home.

Use Week of:

Unit 30 • Session 2
Paul Met Jesus

BIBLE PASSAGE:
Acts 8–9

STORY POINT:
Jesus saved Paul and chose him to spread the gospel.

KEY PASSAGE:
Colossians 1:18

BIG PICTURE QUESTION:
Why does the church exist? The church exists to glorify God by worshiping Him, showing His love, and telling others about Jesus.

INTRODUCE THE STORY
(10–15 MINUTES)
PAGE 174

→

TEACH THE STORY
(25–30 MINUTES)
PAGE 176

→

APPLY THE STORY
(25–30 MINUTES)
PAGE 182

Leaders, grow on the go! Listen to session-by-session training every week on Ministry Grid, Apple Podcasts, Spotify, or LifeWay's Digital Pass: ministrygrid.com/gospelproject | gospelproject.com/podcasts

LEADER Bible Study

Saul was no stranger to religion. He grew up in a religious household. He was a devout Jew who was born in Tarsus (Phil. 3:5) and inherited his Roman citizenship from his father. So when people began talking about this man named Jesus and claiming that He was the promised Messiah, Saul was defensive.

Saul believed strongly in the Jewish faith of his ancestors. He violently persecuted God's church and tried to destroy it. (Gal. 1:13-14) He dragged believers from their houses and put them in prison. He approved of the stoning of Stephen, the first Christian martyr. Saul thought he was doing the right thing by defending Judaism, but God's purposes could not be stopped. As Saul was on his way to arrest believers in Damascus, the Lord stopped him in his tracks.

Jesus revealed Himself to Saul, and Saul was never the same. He was struck blind and led into Damascus, where a believer named Ananias placed his hands on Saul. Suddenly, Saul could see again. Saul was convinced that Jesus is Lord. Saul later described the experience as being like dying and receiving a new life. (Gal. 2:20; 2 Cor. 5:17)

God had a purpose and a plan for Saul. He had set Saul apart before Saul was even born. (Gal. 1:15) God said, "This man is my chosen instrument to take my name to Gentiles, kings, and Israelites" (Acts 9:15).

Jesus changed Saul's life. As you teach kids, clarify that conversion happens when a person recognizes his sin, repents, believes in Jesus, and confesses Jesus as Savior and Lord. Jesus changes a person's heart, and as a result, his life is changed too.

Jesus appeared to Saul and changed him inside and out. Jesus called Saul, who was once an enemy of Christians, to spend the rest of his life telling people the gospel and leading them to trust Jesus as Lord and Savior.

The **BIBLE** Story

Paul Met Jesus
Acts 8–9

After Jesus died, rose from the dead, and ascended to heaven, **people in Jerusalem who believed in Jesus were persecuted**, or treated cruelly **because of their faith.** One of Jesus' followers, **Stephen, was even killed.** A man named **Saul had watched in approval when Stephen was killed. Saul wanted to put an end to the church.** He went into the believers' homes, dragged them out, and put them in jail. Many believers fled the city.

Saul headed to Damascus to arrest believers there, but on the way, a bright light from heaven suddenly flashed around him. Saul fell to the ground. He heard a voice saying, "Saul, Saul, why are you persecuting Me?"

"Who are You, Lord?" Saul asked.

"I am Jesus," He replied. "Get up and go into the city. Then you will be told what you must do."

Saul got up and **opened his eyes, but he couldn't see!** So the men who were traveling with Saul led him by the hand into Damascus.

Ananias (an uh NIGH uhs), a disciple of Jesus, **lived in Damascus. The Lord spoke to Ananias in a vision. He told Ananias to go to the house where Saul was staying.** Ananias knew that Saul had hurt many believers and that he arrested anyone who believed in Jesus. But the Lord said, "Go! I have chosen this man to take my name to Gentiles, kings, and Israelites."

Ananias obeyed. He found Saul and told Saul that Jesus had sent him to help. Ananias put his hands on Saul, and Saul could see again. Saul got up and was baptized. For the next few days, Saul stayed with the believers in Damascus. **He began to go to the synagogues to preach about Jesus.** Saul told the people, "Jesus is the Son of God!"

The people were amazed. They recognized Saul and knew he had wanted to put an end to the church. Now he was one of them! The Jews did not like Saul's message. They planned to kill him, so one night Saul left the city. The disciples helped Saul escape by lowering him down the city wall in a basket.

Saul was also known as Paul.

Christ Connection: Jesus appeared to Paul and changed him inside and out. Jesus Christ came into the world to save sinners. (1 Timothy 1:15) Jesus called Paul, who was once an enemy to Christians, to spend the rest of his life telling people the gospel and leading them to trust in Jesus.

Bible Storytelling Tips

• **Use lighting:** Use a bright flashlight or a spotlight to highlight the bright light Paul saw when Jesus spoke to him.

• **Dress the part:** Wear Bible times clothing and tell the story as if you are a first century believer who heard about Paul's conversion.

INTRODUCE the Story

SESSION TITLE: Paul Met Jesus

BIBLE PASSAGE: Acts 8–9

STORY POINT: Jesus saved Paul and chose him to spread the gospel.

KEY PASSAGE: Colossians 1:18

BIG PICTURE QUESTION: Why does the church exist? The church exists to glorify God by worshiping Him, showing His love, and telling others about Jesus.

Welcome time

Greet each kid as he or she arrives. Use this time to collect the offering, fill out attendance sheets, and help new kids connect to your group. Prompt kids to talk about a time they went on a road trip or vacation with their family and something unexpected occurred. Did they have car trouble? Did someone get stopped at airport security, or lose a suitcase?

SAY • When traveling, there are a lot of things that can go wrong. Today we will learn about a time a man named Saul, also called Paul, had an unexpected delay to his trip. But it turned out to be something going very right!

Activity page (5 minutes)

· "A New Man" activity page, 1 per kid
· pencils or markers

Invite kids to complete the "A New Man" activity page. Guide kids to study the picture of Paul and redraw it using the grid lines as a guide.

SAY • Today we will learn about the time Saul, also called Paul, met Jesus. Although Paul looked the same after meeting Jesus, he had changed completely! In what ways do you think Jesus changed Paul?

Session starter (10 minutes)

· blindfolds, 1 per kid

OPTION 1: Blindfold tag

Select three kids to sit in the middle of the room wearing blindfolds. The other kids must attempt to sneak across the room without alerting the three blindfolded kids. The blindfolded kids must attempt to reach out and tag kids as they cross. Any kids who are tagged will wear blindfolds and join the kids in the middle.

SAY • It was hard to tag anyone when you were blindfolded. Today we will learn about a time Paul, also known as Saul, was blinded while traveling to a city called Damascus. How do you think that happened?

OPTION 2: Red light, green light

LOW PREP

Select a kid to be It. She will stand facing the rest of the group at the far side of the room and announce when the "light" is red or green. The other kids may only move when the light is green. Any kids caught moving when the light is red must return to the starting side of the room. You may add in other light colors with different rules, such as: yellow light–move in slow motion; blue light–hop; purple light–dance; black light–walk backwards.

SAY • It might have felt frustrating to be on your way across the room when a red light stopped you. Today we will learn about a time Paul, also known as Saul, was stopped in the middle of his journey. Who do you think stopped him, and why?

Transition to teach the story

TEACH the Story

SESSION TITLE: Paul Met Jesus

BIBLE PASSAGE: Acts 8–9

STORY POINT: Jesus saved Paul and chose him to spread the gospel.

KEY PASSAGE: Colossians 1:18

BIG PICTURE QUESTION: Why does the church exist? The church exists to glorify God by worshiping Him, showing His love, and telling others about Jesus.

Countdown

· countdown video

Show the countdown video as you transition to teach the story. Set it to end as the session begins.

Introduce the session (3 minutes)

· leader attire

[Leader enters wearing khaki shorts and a polo shirt, with a whistle hanging from a lanyard around her neck.]

Tip: If you prefer not to use themed content or characters, adapt or omit this introduction.

LEADER • Hey everyone, welcome back to the field. I'm glad you are here for soccer tryouts and lessons about Jesus. You know, I had a kid try out just now who used to play for another team. It was the strangest thing. Last season, when he played for the Turf Burners, he was a bit of a mess.

I don't mean how he looked. Soccer can be a messy sport, so all the kids are covered in grass stains and dirt smears. No, I mean, he was a very aggressive, downright mean player. He had a lot of talent, but very poor sportsmanship. He actually twisted the ankle of our star player while slide tackling to steal the ball. The referee called the foul, but we still lost since our star couldn't play anymore

Anyway, that's all just to give you a little context

for what happened yesterday. He came and apologized for last year, said his coach cut him from his team, and asked if he could try out for ours. He was kind, considerate, polite, and listened well to my instructions. It was as though he was a new kid! I'm not sure exactly what changed, but I'm glad to have him on our team now.

You know, that reminds me of our Bible story. It is about a man who no one would have expected to follow Jesus, and how he ended up doing just that!

Big picture question (1 minute)

LEADER • Last week we asked and answered a big picture question—*Why does the church exist? The church exists to glorify God by worshiping Him, showing His love, and telling others about Jesus.* That means that Jesus didn't save us for no reason. We are saved so that we can be a part of God's mission on earth. God is the greatest treasure, and deserves all glory and worship. As the church, we work to glorify God in everything we do and help others learn to glorify God as well.

Giant timeline (1 minute)

Show the giant timeline. Point to individual Bible stories as you review.

· Giant Timeline

LEADER • Last week we learned about Philip. The Holy Spirit led Philip to tell the Ethiopian man about Jesus. That Ethiopian official believed the gospel and was baptized. This week, we will learn about the unlikely conversion of another man. His name was Saul and he hated Christians.

Tell the Bible story (10 minutes)

- Bibles
- "Paul Met Jesus" video
- Big Picture Question Poster
- Bible Story Picture Poster
- Story Point Poster

Open your Bible to Acts 8–9. Use the Bible storytelling tips on the Bible story page to help you tell the story, or show the Bible story video "Paul Met Jesus."

LEADER • Saul, also known as Paul, didn't just dislike Christians. He hated them. In fact, he watched while the religious leaders killed Stephen—and Paul thought it was good for them to do that. When we understand how cruel Paul was before he met Jesus, we can see how merciful, gracious, and powerful God really is.

No one but God could cause such a big shift in a man's life. **Jesus saved Paul and chose him to spread the gospel**. As you can imagine, the first believers who met with Paul were concerned. Ananias was afraid to even go see him at first! But after Paul regained his physical sight, it became clear that the Holy Spirit had come into his heart to give him spiritual sight as well. Paul was a new person, completely changed by the power of the gospel.

That's true for everyone who repents and believes the gospel. It always changes us from the inside out. The Bible teaches that we become new creations! In fact, the man who wrote that was Paul! This man, who hated Christians and wanted to see all of them arrested or killed, became one of the primary writers of the New Testament! There's an entire division named for the writings the Holy Spirit inspired him to produce: Paul's Letters. No one is too sinful or too evil to be saved by God's perfect goodness, grace, and mercy.

Christ connection

LEADER • Jesus appeared to Paul and changed him inside and out. Jesus Christ came into the world to save sinners. (1 Timothy 1:15) Jesus called Paul, who was once an enemy to Christians, to spend the rest of his life telling people the gospel and leading them to trust in Jesus.

Questions from kids video (3 minutes)

Show the "Unit 30, Session 2" questions from kids video. Prompt kids to think about whether or not they have put their faith in Jesus. Guide them to discuss ways God has changed them or believers they know.

Missions moment (3 minutes)

Print the "Missionaries Around the World" printable and display the pictures around the room. Invite strong readers to read the captions. Allow all the kids to walk around the room to look at the pictures.

LEADER • Jesus saved Paul from his sins and chose him to spread the gospel. These missionaries were also chosen by Jesus for a special task of living in another country and telling the people there about Jesus.

Pray, thanking God for missionaries—including those your church supports—who spread the gospel.

Key passage (5 minutes)

Show the key passage poster. Lead the boys and girls to read together Colossians 1:18. Then sing the key passage song.

LEADER • After becoming a Christian, Paul wanted everyone to understand how wonderful Jesus is. Paul knew that his sins against God and the church were

Note: You may use this opportunity to use Scripture and the guide provided to explain how to become a Christian. Make sure kids know when and where they can ask questions.

· "Unit 30, Session 2" Questions from Kids video

· "Missionaries Around the World" printable

· Key Passage Poster
· "First Place in Everything (Colossians 1:18)" song

too great for him to deal with, but he also knew that nothing is too big for God to deal with. When Jesus is the most important person in our lives, we can live on mission to glorify Him in the whole world.

Sing (4 minutes)

· "One Foundation" song

LEADER • Jesus is our greatest treasure. He deserves first place in everything, because He is the foundation of our lives and faith.

Sing together "One Foundation."

Pray (2 minutes)

Invite kids to pray before dismissing to apply the story.

LEADER • Father, thank You that no sin is too great for You to forgive. Help us to know that there is hope for everyone, and give us boldness to share that hope with each person we meet. Amen.

Dismiss to apply the story

The Gospel: God's Plan for Me

Ask kids if they have ever heard the word *gospel*. Clarify that the word *gospel* means "good news." It is the message about Christ, the kingdom of God, and salvation. Use the following guide to share the gospel with kids.

God rules. Explain to kids that the Bible tells us God created everything, and He is in charge of everything. Invite a volunteer to read Genesis 1:1 from the Bible. Read Revelation 4:11 or Colossians 1:16-17 aloud and explain what these verses mean.

We sinned. Tell kids that since the time of Adam and Eve, everyone has chosen to disobey God. (Romans 3:23) The Bible calls this sin. Because God is holy, God cannot be around sin. Sin separates us from God and deserves God's punishment of death. (Romans 6:23)

God provided. Choose a child to read John 3:16 aloud. Say that God sent His Son, Jesus, the perfect solution to our sin problem, to rescue us from the punishment we deserve. It's something we, as sinners, could never earn on our own. Jesus alone saves us. Read and explain Ephesians 2:8-9.

Jesus gives. Share with kids that Jesus lived a perfect life, died on the cross for our sins, and rose again. Because Jesus gave up His life for us, we can be welcomed into God's family for eternity. This is the best gift ever! Read Romans 5:8; 2 Corinthians 5:21; or 1 Peter 3:18.

We respond. Tell kids that they can respond to Jesus. Read Romans 10:9-10,13. Review these aspects of our response: Believe in your heart that Jesus alone saves you through what He's already done on the cross. Repent, turning from self and sin to Jesus. Tell God and others that your faith is in Jesus.

Offer to talk with any child who is interested in responding to Jesus. Provide *I'm a Christian Now!* for new Christians to take home and complete with their families.

APPLY the Story

SESSION TITLE: Paul Met Jesus

BIBLE PASSAGE: Acts 8–9

STORY POINT: Jesus saved Paul and chose him to spread the gospel.

KEY PASSAGE: Colossians 1:18

BIG PICTURE QUESTION: Why does the church exist? The church exists to glorify God by worshiping Him, showing His love, and telling others about Jesus.

Key passage activity (5 minutes)

· Key Passage Poster
· paper
· markers, crayons, or colored pencils

Provide each kid with a sheet of paper and markers, crayons, or colored pencils. Direct the kids to write the key passage multiple time, switching colors each time, so that their writing looks like a rainbow. Then read the key passage aloud together.

SAY • When Paul met Jesus, it changed everything about his life. Paul went from hating Christians to writing letters to help them love and obey Jesus more! This key passage is from one of Paul's letters. He wanted believers to remember that Jesus is the most valuable treasure. Jesus is the leader of the church, and He is everything we need.

Discussion & Bible skills (10 minutes)

· Bibles, 1 per kid
· Story Point Poster
· Small Group Timeline and Map Set (005802970, optional)

Distribute a Bible to each kid. Help them find Acts 8–9. Ask the kids which division of the New Testament Acts is in. (*History*) Ask the kids how many books are in it, and which division comes before and after this division. (*only one; Gospels, Paul's Letters*) Then, consider showing the New Testament Israel Map to point out the location of Damascus, where Paul was traveling in the story. (*A8*)

Younger Kids Leader Guide
Unit 30 • Session 2

Ask the following questions. Lead the group to discuss:

Option: Retell or review the Bible story using the bolded text of the Bible story script.

1. Why was Paul traveling to Damascus? (*to arrest and persecute Christians, Acts 9:1-2*)

2. What did Jesus ask Paul? (*"Why are you persecuting me?" Acts 9:4*)

3. What did Paul do when his sight was restored? (*preached about Jesus in the synagogue, Acts 9:20*)

4. Why do you think God chose to use Paul to spread the gospel? *Help the kids think through what we learn about God's power from His choice to use Paul. Discuss our tendency to see some people as "too bad" for salvation. Remind them that all have sinned, and God's power and love are greater than the power of sin in our lives. Choosing Paul was a way for God to show His power and control of all things.*

5. Can you think of anyone you would be shocked to learn became a Christian? *Encourage kids to be honest and open about their thoughts. Remind them that God loves each person, and that Jesus came to save all sinners. Help them see that all sin is enough to earn death and separation from God.*

6. What are ways you think you need to change to be more like Jesus? *Lead kids to discuss their own need for grace and mercy. Help them talk through their flaws and remind them that the Holy Spirit changes all believers over time to be more like Jesus.*

SAY • **Jesus saved Paul and chose him to spread the gospel**. Paul hated Christians and wanted to see all of them arrested and even killed. When Jesus changed his heart, he became a wonderful tool in God's hands, and spread the gospel all over. How might God use us in His plan to reach the world?

The Church Grew

- "Missionary Tools" printable
- guitar (optional)
- shovel (optional)
- stethoscope (optional)
- cell phone (optional)

Tip: Use this activity option to reinforce the missions moment found in Teach the Story.

LOW PREP

Activity choice (10 minutes)

OPTION 1: Missionary tools

Print and cut apart the "Missionary Tools" printable. Form four groups of kids and give one card to each kid. Ask them to think of ways a missionary could use the item on their card to share the gospel. Be prepared to offer examples to any groups that get stuck. You may choose to use actual items, if you have them available.

SAY • Missionaries around the world use many different tools to serve people and spread the gospel. But the Bible is the most important tool. Missionaries want people to know that the Word of God teaches us how to know Jesus and be saved. Any tool a missionary uses will eventually point to Jesus.

OPTION 2: Chain tag

Select a kid to be *It*. He will tag other kids to link arms with them, making them part of the chain. Those kids may then tag other kids to grow the chain. The game ends when all the kids are part of the chain.

SAY • That was fun! At first it may have seemed tough to grow the human chain, but the more kids who joined, the easier it was to reach more kids. That reminds me of our story.

Jesus saved Paul and chose him to share the gospel. Though Paul was only one man, God used him in His plans to share the gospel all over the world! Paul quickly began to tell others and select more leaders who would also spread the gospel. As we continue learning about God's plan in the weeks to come, you will see how God used one person to grow the church bigger and bigger as more and more people began to share the gospel.

Reflection and prayer (5 minutes)

Distribute a sheet of paper to each child. Ask the kids to write about or draw a picture to answer the following questions:

- What does this story teach me about God or about the gospel?
- What does this story teach me about myself?
- Whom can I tell about this story?

Make sure to send the sheets home with kids alongside the activity page so that parents can see what their kids have been learning.

If time remains, take prayer requests or allow kids to complete the Bible story coloring page provided with this session. Pray for your group.

· pencils and crayons
· paper
· Bible Story Coloring Page, 1 per kid

Tip: Give parents this week's Big Picture Cards for Families to allow families to interact with the biblical content at home.

Unit 30 · Session 3
New Life in Jesus

BIBLE PASSAGE:
Colossians 2–3

STORY POINT:
Jesus gives new life to people who trust in Him.

KEY PASSAGE:
Colossians 1:18

BIG PICTURE QUESTION:
Why does the church exist? The church exists to glorify God by worshiping Him, showing His love, and telling others about Jesus.

INTRODUCE THE STORY
(10–15 MINUTES)
PAGE 190

→

TEACH THE STORY
(25–30 MINUTES)
PAGE 192

→

APPLY THE STORY
(25–30 MINUTES)
PAGE 198

Leaders, grow on the go! Listen to session-by-session training every week on Ministry Grid, Apple Podcasts, Spotify, or LifeWay's Digital Pass: ministrygrid.com/gospelproject | gospelproject.com/podcasts

LEADER Bible Study

Paul wrote his letter to the Colossians while he was imprisoned in Rome. At this point, Paul had not yet visited the church at Colossae. The church was established by Epaphras, who reported to Paul that the church was facing troubles with false teachers. Paul wanted to put an end to the false teaching and remind the believers of who Jesus really is. Key to this letter is Paul's teaching about how the gospel affects how we live.

As you teach kids from Colossians 2–3, focus on some of the main points Paul makes. First, God changes us when we trust in Jesus. The Bible describes us apart from Jesus as "enemies of God" (Rom. 5:10) and "dead" in our sins (Eph. 2:1). Jesus rescued us from sin and death by dying on the cross and rising again. Jesus gives new life to people who trust in Him.

Second, following Jesus means living for Him. Jesus is our reason for living, and He gives us power to live in a way that honors Him. Jesus adopts us into His family and makes us new! We respond to the good news of the gospel by submitting to Jesus as Lord and Savior.

Finally, Jesus calls us to turn away from our sinful ways and live in a way that honors Him. Paul contrasts an earthly way of thinking with a godly way of thinking. The old, sinful way of living (the "old self") is characterized by anger, wrath, hatred, lies, and filthy language. Paul wrote that living for Jesus means putting away the evil, selfish ways of the world and living like Jesus by loving God and loving others.

In Jesus, we have power to live in a new, godly way. This way (the "new self") is marked by compassion, kindness, humility, gentleness, patience, and love. Paul says believers should "put on" these things. As we grow in this new way of living, God is making us more like His Son.

The **BIBLE** Story

New Life in Jesus
Colossians 2–3

Paul became a Christian a few years after Jesus died and rose again. He joined the early church **and traveled around, sharing the gospel with others. Paul often wrote letters to churches** when he was away from them. **In his letter to the church at Colossae** (koh LAHS sih), **Paul explained how people should live as followers of Jesus.**

"As you received Jesus Christ as Lord, continue to live in Him," Paul wrote. **"Build your life on Him. Be strong in your faith and always be thankful."**

Paul told the believers to be careful about who they listened to. Sometimes the words of the world sound good and right, but they are not based on God's truth. Jesus died to set us free from the ways of the world.

Paul wrote, "Think about godly things, not earthly things. When you trusted in Jesus, you died with Him. Now you live in Him, so turn away from the ways of the world. Put away anger, wrath, hatred, lies, and filthy language from your mouth. Do not lie to one another. You used to live this way, but Jesus has given you a new life."

Paul said that God is making us more like Jesus. In this new life, no one is more important than anyone else; we all belong to Jesus.

Younger Kids Leader Guide
Unit 30 • Session 3

Paul wrote, "You are God's chosen ones, holy and dearly loved. **Put on compassion, kindness, humility, gentleness, and patience. Bear with one another and forgive one another** because the Lord has forgiven you. Above all, put on love. Let the peace of Jesus rule your hearts, and be thankful."

Paul encouraged believers to remember Jesus' teachings and obey them, teaching and encouraging one another. "Sing to God with thankfulness in your hearts," Paul wrote. **"Children, obey your parents because this pleases God. And whatever you do, do everything in the name of Jesus, giving thanks to God** the Father through Him."

Christ Connection: God changes us when we trust in Jesus. He adopts us into His family and makes us new! Jesus calls us to turn away from our sinful ways and live in a way that honors Him.

...**tory**

INT...to people who trust in Him.

SESS...

BIB...hy does the church exist? The church exists to ...ing Him, showing His love, and telling others

Welcome time

Greet each kid as he or she arrives. Use this time to collect the offering, fill out attendance sheets, and help new kids connect to your group. Prompt kids to talk about their favorite outfit, article of clothing, or costume they've ever worn.

SAY • Sometimes your favorite clothes might be something super comfy. Or maybe you love a special sports jersey with the number worn by your favorite player. Maybe you like a certain costume that helps you pretend you are a fictional character that you like. Today we will learn about something the Bible tells us to "put away" and something else we should "put on" like clothing. But it's not actual clothes!

Activity page (5 minutes)

· "Put Away or Put On?" activity page, 1 per kid
· pencils or markers

Invite kids to complete the "Put Away or Put On?" activity page. Kids will sort the words from the bank into the correct side of the T-chart.

SAY • The Bible tells us how to live. Some traits we should work to display, and other traits we should avoid. The Holy Spirit produces good traits in our lives.

Session starter (10 minutes)

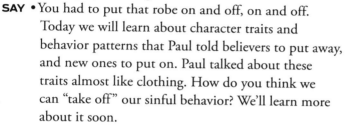

OPTION 1: Robe relay

· bathrobes, 2

Form two teams of kids. Instruct them to line up on one side of the room and provide each team with a bathrobe. Each kid will take turns putting on his team's robe, walking to the end of the room and back, removing the robe, and handing it to the next player to do the same. The first team to send each player through the race wins.

SAY • You had to put that robe on and off, on and off. Today we will learn about character traits and behavior patterns that Paul told believers to put away, and new ones to put on. Paul talked about these traits almost like clothing. How do you think we can "take off" our sinful behavior? We'll learn more about it soon.

OPTION 2: Tennis ball crash

· tennis balls, 2
· plastic cups, 6

Form two teams of kids. Provide each team with a tennis ball. In the center of the room, stack six plastic cups in a pyramid shape. Challenge the team's to take turns rolling their tennis balls to hit the stack. Each time the tower is knocked over, reset it and continue playing. Ensure each kid gets a chance to roll the ball.

SAY • Those were some great *collisions*. A collision is like a crash, when two objects run into each other while moving. That's different from a Colossian, who is a person from the ancient city of Colossae. (koh LAHS sih) Paul wrote a letter to the Colossians, believers in Colossae. That letter became the book of Colossians, which we will study today.

Transition to teach the story

The Church Grew

TEACH the Story

SESSION TITLE: New Life in Jesus

BIBLE PASSAGE: Colossians 2–3

STORY POINT: Jesus gives new life to people who trust in Him.

KEY PASSAGE: Colossians 1:18

BIG PICTURE QUESTION: Why does the church exist? The church exists to glorify God by worshiping Him, showing His love, and telling others about Jesus.

Countdown

· countdown video

Show the countdown video as you transition to teach the story. Set it to end as the session begins.

Introduce the session (3 minutes)

· leader attire

[Leader enters wearing khaki shorts and a polo shirt, with a whistle hanging from a lanyard around her neck.]

Tip: If you prefer not to use themed content or characters, adapt or omit this introduction.

LEADER • Hey there kids! It's good to see you all again. Soccer try-outs have been going really well. The training has been pretty intense, but it has been worth it. I've seen a lot of growth in the recruits, and by the time I have the final roster, I'm sure all the players will be ready for anything.

I will say that the one major downside to all the training is having gear wear out. Thankfully, there's a generous local business that has offered to buy us new uniforms in exchange for putting an ad for his shop in the soccer league newsletter. So now, we all get to put away our old gear that's falling apart and put on new gear that is ready to help us win games!

You know, this actually makes me think of our Bible story this session. Did you know that

Christians also have certain traits that are old and need to be replaced? Paul wrote about it in one of his letters to a church in Colossae. I'll tell you about it.

Big picture question (1 minute)

LEADER • As we've been learning about the early church, it has been important to discuss a special big picture question and answer. *Why does the church exist? The church exists to glorify God by worshiping Him, showing His love, and telling others about Jesus.* Jesus saves us, but not so we can sit around and be happy we are saved. We should feel extreme joy because of salvation, but that joy will naturally push us to glorify God by serving Him and spreading the message of the gospel. As the church grows, more people glorify God, and that's what we were created to do all along!

Giant timeline (1 minute)

Show the giant timeline. Point to individual Bible stories as you review.

· Giant Timeline

LEADER • Two weeks ago, we learned that **the Holy Spirit led Philip to tell the Ethiopian man about Jesus**. Last week, we heard the amazing story of Paul's conversion. **Jesus saved Paul and chose him to spread the gospel.** God used Paul to start many churches and to instruct churches in how to fulfill their purpose to worship God, show His love, and tell others about him. This week, we are going to learn a bit about one of the churches Paul planted, as well as the letter he wrote to help them love and obey God more fully.

The Church Grew

Tell the Bible story (10 minutes)

· Bibles
· "New Life in Jesus" video
· Big Picture Question Poster
· Bible Story Picture Poster
· Story Point Poster

Open your Bible to Colossians 2–3. Use the Bible storytelling tips on the Bible story page to help you tell the story, or show the Bible story video "New Life in Jesus."

LEADER • The messages of the world can often sound pretty good to us. "You get what you deserve;" "do what makes you happy;" "you have to look out for yourself;" "follow your heart" …

But those messages are not what Jesus wants for us. What we deserve is death because of our sin. What makes us happy is very often bad for us. If we only look out for ourselves, we live selfishly. And the Bible teaches that our hearts are tricky and will lead us to chase after sin.

Paul's letter to the Colossians helped them see that they needed to radically change their lives to match God's plans for them. We can't say we have faith and then go on living selfishly. That's not how it works! When we repent and believe the gospel, the Holy Spirit lives in us and transforms us to look more like Jesus. That means loving even our enemies, caring for the needs of other people, giving generously, and following God instead of our sinful hearts.

Christ connection

Note: You may use this opportunity to use Scripture and the guide provided to explain how to become a Christian. Make sure kids know when and where they can ask questions.

LEADER • Turning from sin isn't always easy, but it is always worth it. Every sin that seems fun or easy will end up hurting us and making our lives harder, eventually. God changes us when we trust in Jesus. He adopts us into His family and makes us new! Jesus calls us to turn away from our sinful ways and live in a way that honors Him.

Questions from kids video (3 minutes)

Show the "Unit 30, Session 3" questions from kids video. Prompt kids to think about why believers still sin sometimes. Guide them to discuss how they feel about God's promise to help us overcome temptation.

- "Unit 30, Session 3" Questions from Kids video

Missions moment (3 minutes)

Play the "Baptisms Around the World" video. You may choose to allow any kids in your group who have been baptized to describe their experiences.

- "Baptisms Around the World" missions video

LEADER • Missionaries get to see how Jesus gives new life to people who were dead in sin. It's great to see how people obey Jesus' command to follow Him through baptism, which is a way to tell other people that they have new life in Jesus.

Key passage (5 minutes)

Show the key passage poster. Lead the boys and girls to read together Colossians 1:18. Then sing the key passage song.

- Key Passage Poster
- "First Place in Everything (Colossians 1:18)" song

LEADER • Our key passage comes from the very letter we are studying today. Paul wanted believers to treasure Jesus more than anything. When we make Jesus the most important part of our lives, the Holy Spirit changes us to be more like Him. That makes putting away sin and putting on holiness easier and easier each day.

Sing (4 minutes)

LEADER • When we live for Jesus, the mission to make disciples becomes an important part of our lives. Let's worship Him for helping us live on mission.

- "This Is Where the Mission Begins" song

Sing together "This Is Where the Mission Begins."

Pray (2 minutes)

Invite kids to pray before dismissing to apply the story.

LEADER • Father, our hearts are broken by sin, and it's only Your power that can fix us. Help us to live for Your glory. Give us boldness to pursue You no matter what. Help us put away old sins and put on holiness that honors Jesus before everything else in our lives. Amen.

Dismiss to apply the story

The Gospel: God's Plan for Me

Ask kids if they have ever heard the word *gospel*. Clarify that the word *gospel* means "good news." It is the message about Christ, the kingdom of God, and salvation. Use the following guide to share the gospel with kids.

God rules. Explain to kids that the Bible tells us God created everything, and He is in charge of everything. Invite a volunteer to read Genesis 1:1 from the Bible. Read Revelation 4:11 or Colossians 1:16-17 aloud and explain what these verses mean.

We sinned. Tell kids that since the time of Adam and Eve, everyone has chosen to disobey God. (Romans 3:23) The Bible calls this sin. Because God is holy, God cannot be around sin. Sin separates us from God and deserves God's punishment of death. (Romans 6:23)

God provided. Choose a child to read John 3:16 aloud. Say that God sent His Son, Jesus, the perfect solution to our sin problem, to rescue us from the punishment we deserve. It's something we, as sinners, could never earn on our own. Jesus alone saves us. Read and explain Ephesians 2:8-9.

Jesus gives. Share with kids that Jesus lived a perfect life, died on the cross for our sins, and rose again. Because Jesus gave up His life for us, we can be welcomed into God's family for eternity. This is the best gift ever! Read Romans 5:8; 2 Corinthians 5:21; or 1 Peter 3:18.

We respond. Tell kids that they can respond to Jesus. Read Romans 10:9-10,13. Review these aspects of our response: Believe in your heart that Jesus alone saves you through what He's already done on the cross. Repent, turning from self and sin to Jesus. Tell God and others that your faith is in Jesus.

Offer to talk with any child who is interested in responding to Jesus. Provide *I'm a Christian Now!* for new Christians to take home and complete with their families.

APPLY the Story

SESSION TITLE: New Life in Jesus

BIBLE PASSAGE: Colossians 2–3

STORY POINT: Jesus gives new life to people who trust in Him.

KEY PASSAGE: Colossians 1:18

BIG PICTURE QUESTION: Why does the church exist? The church exists to glorify God by worshiping Him, showing His love, and telling others about Jesus.

Key passage activity (5 minutes)

· Key Passage Poster
· sticky notes
· pen

Write each word of phrase of the key passage on a separate sticky note. Place a sticky note on each kid's back. Challenge the kids to work together to stand in the correct order without reading the words or phrases on their individual backs. Invite a volunteer to say the key passage from memory. Thank each kid for her efforts and encourage all the kids to continue working to memorize the passage.

SAY • Paul wrote these words in his letter to the believers living in Colossae. Paul wanted them to know that Jesus is the leader and most important part of the church. We all must love and obey Him as part of the church. *Why does the church exist? The church exists to glorify God by worshiping Him, showing His love, and telling others about Jesus.*

Discussion & Bible skills (10 minutes)

· Bibles, 1 per kid
· Story Point Poster
· Small Group Timeline
  and Map Set
  (005802970, optional)

Distribute a Bible to each kid. Help them find Colossians 2–3. Remind kids that Colossian is part of the Paul's Letters division of the New Testament. Use the New Testament Mediterranean Map to point out where Colossa was located. (*E7*)

Ask the following questions. Lead the group to discuss:

Option: Retell or review the Bible story using the bolded text of the Bible story script.

1. What did Paul tell believers to continue to do? (*to walk in Christ, Col. 2:6*)

2. What should believers think about? (*heavenly things, Col. 3:1-2*)

3. What did Paul tell children to do? (*obey their parents; Col. 3:20*)

4. How does God make us new? *Discuss the immediate change that takes place in our standing before God when we believe the gospel. Remind kids that there is also a gradual change in our lives as the Holy Spirit makes us more and more like Jesus over time. Teach the kids the words justification and sanctification to describe these changes, the immediate and the gradual, respectively.*

5. Why does God make us new? *Talk kids through God's desire to show us love and mercy. Remind them that we were created to glorify God by enjoying His goodness. Explain that sin prevents us from doing what we were made to do. God makes us new so that we can glorify Him as we were supposed to all along. That is how we experience the most joy in life.*

6. Why is love so important for believers? *Guide kids to think through the ways all of God's commands center on loving Him and loving people. Love for God motivates us to love people. Remind them that when we love others, we want what is best for them; we will want them to live with God as we do.*

SAY • **Jesus gives new life to people who trust in Him.** The life Jesus gives is the only way to experience true joy and peace. The Holy Spirit helps us to live in a way that honors God.

LOW PREP

· "Exploring Baptism" printable
· scissors
· tape

Tip: Use this activity option to reinforce the missions moment found in Teach the Story.

Activity choice (10 minutes)

OPTION 1: Exploring baptism

Print and cut apart the "Exploring Baptism" printable. Hang the photos around the room, and distribute the captions among smaller groups of kids. Challenge the kids to work together to match the descriptions to the pictures.

SAY • Christians around the world are baptized in many different ways. Many believers do not have access to indoor plumbing or a special baptismal in a church. But they still obey Jesus' command to baptize new believers. When they believe in Jesus, they have new life with Him. Baptism cannot give you new life, but it is a way Christians show the world the new life Jesus gave them when they believed the gospel and had faith in Him.

OPTION 2: Focus pocus

· masking tape
· paper scraps
· pens or markers

Use masking tape to make a target shape on the floor. Provide each kid with a scrap of paper. Kids will write their name on the paper, then wad it up and use it as a ball.

In the first round of the game, ask each kid to toss their ball onto the target while facing away from the target. Use a small bit of tape to record where each kid's paper wad landed. In the next round, allow the kids to aim by looking at the target while they toss their wads. Note which kids were able to get closer to the center of the target in the second round.

SAY • If you don't focus on the target, it is nearly impossible to hit the target. That seems simple enough, right? In our lives, we often forget to focus on Jesus, and then wonder why it is difficult to live our lives for His glory. Paul reminded believers that they needed to focus on Jesus, setting their minds on things above—things that have to do with God and His commands. We must do the same.

We set our minds on things above when we study our Bibles, pray, and learn about God with the church community. When we have faith in Jesus, obeying Him becomes easier the more we focus on Him.

Reflection and prayer (5 minutes)

Distribute a sheet of paper to each child. Ask the kids to write about or draw a picture to answer the following questions:

- What does this story teach me about God or about the gospel?
- What does this story teach me about myself?
- Whom can I tell about this story?

Make sure to send the sheets home with kids alongside the activity page so that parents can see what their kids have been learning.

If time remains, take prayer requests or allow kids to complete the Bible story coloring page provided with this session. Pray for your group.

- pencils and crayons
- paper
- Bible Story Coloring Page, 1 per kid

Tip: Give parents this week's Big Picture Cards for Families to allow families to interact with the biblical content at home.

Unit 30 · Session 4
Guarding the Truth

BIBLE PASSAGE:
2 Corinthians 11

STORY POINT:
God gives us power to stand up for the gospel.

KEY PASSAGE:
Colossians 1:18

BIG PICTURE QUESTION:
Why does the church exist? The church exists to glorify God by worshiping Him showing His love, and telling others about Jesus.

INTRODUCE THE STORY
(10–15 MINUTES)
PAGE 206

→

TEACH THE STORY
(25–30 MINUTES)
PAGE 208

→

APPLY THE STORY
(25–30 MINUTES)
PAGE 214

Leaders, grow on the go! Listen to session-by-session training every week on Ministry Grid, Apple Podcasts, Spotify, or LifeWay's Digital Pass: ministrygrid.com/gospelproject | gospelproject.com/podcasts

LEADER Bible Study

In New Testament times, Corinth was an important city in ancient Greece. About eighteen years after Jesus' death on the cross, Paul preached the gospel to the Corinthians and established the church there. (See Acts 18.) He stayed in Corinth for at least 18 months.

In his first letter to the Corinthians, Paul wrote to help believers solve some problems within the church. In his second letter, written just a few weeks later, Paul wrote to encourage the church and to assure them that God loved them—even when they had troubles. Of all Paul's letters in the New Testament, none reveals his heart as much as 2 Corinthians. In it, Paul showed his passion for Christ as he fiercely defended his ministry against false teachings.

Paul wrote of the dangers he faced as a disciple of Christ—stonings, beatings, imprisonment, hunger, and hardship. But he also wrote of the comfort and the strength to endure that Jesus gives to those who trust in Him. Nothing could keep Paul from sharing the good news of Jesus—a lesson for the believers at Corinth and for all believers everywhere.

4

As you teach from 2 Corinthians 11, emphasize that God gives us power to stand up for the gospel. Paul cared about the believers in Corinth, and he wanted them to be faithful to Jesus and remember the gospel. Paul may not have been an eloquent speaker like those who preached lies, but he refused to back down. Paul suffered and nearly died to share the gospel.

Second Corinthians teaches us that sharing Jesus with the world is not always easy. There will always be some who try to stop the good news from spreading. But our job as believers is to follow and obey Jesus no matter what. Like Paul, we guard the truth because God, the Father of the Lord Jesus, deserves to be praised.

The BIBLE Story

Guarding the Truth
2 Corinthians 11

Paul had shared the good news about Jesus in Corinth. Many people believed the gospel, and they began meeting together as a church. **After Paul left, he heard that the believers in Corinth were turning away from the gospel.** Other **people had come and taught them things that weren't true.** These teachers led the Corinthians away from the one true gospel, and Paul was worried. **So Paul wrote a letter to the church.**

"Listen," **Paul wrote, "I care about you. I want you to be faithful to Jesus and remember the gospel."** Paul **knew that the people had been tricked by the false teachers,** like the serpent in the garden of Eden had tricked Eve. Eve had everything she needed, but she believed the serpent's lie and disobeyed God. **The Corinthian believers had everything they needed—the good news of the gospel—yet they were turning away to listen to wrong teaching.**

"I'm not a great speaker," Paul admitted, "but I know what I'm talking about." **Paul relied on God's power to share the gospel. He spent his life sharing the good news, even though it meant facing suffering. Paul didn't share the gospel to get something** from those who listened; he told them about Jesus because he loved them!

Paul wrote, "I won't back down. False teachers are trying to spread different messages so that the good news about Jesus won't go out. These teachers are against God, and they're only trying to take advantage of you."

Paul spoke up because he knew the truth. "If anyone deserves to be listened to, it's me. I've worked hard, been thrown in jail and beaten, and nearly died to share the gospel." God had chosen Paul and had changed his life. Paul knew his suffering was worth it, and he wasn't going to give up. "I do all of this because God, the Father of the Lord Jesus, deserves to be praised."

Christ Connection: Sharing Jesus with the world is not always easy. There will always be some who try to stop the good news from spreading. God calls believers to follow and obey Jesus no matter what.

Bible Storytelling Tips

- **Display a map:** Use the New Testament Mediterrenean Map or a larger world map to point out Corinth (in modern day Greece west of Athens).
- **Vary your voice:** Shift the sound of your voice to distinguish between quotes and explanations..

INTRODUCE the Story

SESSION TITLE: Guarding the Truth

BIBLE PASSAGE: 2 Corinthians 11

STORY POINT: God gives us power to stand up for the gospel.

KEY PASSAGE: Colossians 1:18

BIG PICTURE QUESTION: Why does the church exist? The church exists to glorify God by worshiping Him, showing His love, and telling others about Jesus.

Welcome time

Greet each kid as he or she arrives. Use this time to collect the offering, fill out attendance sheets, and help new kids connect to your group. Prompt kids to talk about a time they faced bullying or stood up to a bully. If any kid discloses abuse or neglect, report such claims to the proper authorities according to the law where you live and your ministry's policies.

SAY • It's never fun to feel bullied. We are called to love all people, and when you see someone being bullied, it's important to stand up to help victims. Today we will learn about a group of people who were lying to believers, trying to get them to believe things that were not true. Paul wrote to defend the truth!

Activity page (5 minutes)

· "The Real Deal" activity page, 1 per kid
· pencils or markers

Invite kids to complete the "The Real Deal" activity page. Instruct kids to study the different pictures of Paul to find the one that is different from the rest.

SAY • When false teachers spread lies in the church, Paul had to defend the truth and his own reputation as an apostle chosen by God. Paul was the real deal!

Session starter (10 minutes)

OPTION 1: Never have I ever

Guide the kids to sit in a circle. Each kid will hold up three fingers. Select a kid to go first. She will say "never have I ever …" and complete the sentence with an activity she has never done—such as eaten a grapefruit, ridden a roller coaster, or pet a snake. Each kid who has done that activity must put one finger down. Then the next kid will have a chance to make a "never have I ever" statement. Play in this way until only one kid has any fingers up. That kid wins.

SAY • You all have done a lot of different and interesting things. Today we will learn about a time Paul listed some of the many sufferings he faced as a result of telling people about Jesus. Why do you think Paul would talk about all the things he did to spread the truth about Jesus?

OPTION 2: Guarding the goals

Use traffic cones to mark two goals on either side of the room. Form two teams of kids and place a beach ball in the center of the room. Instruct teams to walk on their knees. When you say go, teams must work together to earn points by rolling the ball into the opposing team's goal. After a few minutes, declare the team with the most points the winner.

· traffic cones, 4
· beach ball

SAY • One good strategy in that game was to make sure someone stayed near the goal to guard it, like a goalie or keeper in soccer. Today we will learn about a time Paul wrote a letter to "guard" Christians from believing lies told by false teachers. What kind of lies do you think Paul may have guarded against?

Transition to teach the story

TEACH the Story

SESSION TITLE: Guarding the Truth

BIBLE PASSAGE: 2 Corinthians 11

STORY POINT: God gives us power to stand up for the gospel.

KEY PASSAGE: Colossians 1:18

BIG PICTURE QUESTION: Why does the church exist? The church exists to glorify God by worshiping Him, showing His love, and telling others about Jesus.

Countdown

· countdown video

Show the countdown video as you transition to teach the story. Set it to end as the session begins.

Introduce the session (3 minutes)

· leader attire

[Leader enters wearing khaki shorts and a polo shirt, with a whistle hanging from a lanyard around her neck.]

Tip: If you prefer not to use themed content or characters, adapt or omit this introduction.

LEADER • Hey everyone. I'm glad you could make it today. This is the last week of the team tryouts. At this point I've got most of my roster filled up. All I need now is one very special position filled: the goalie.

Depending on who you ask, the goalie might be the single most important position on a soccer team. A good goalie will often mean the difference between winning a game and losing it. No matter how good the rest of your team may be, if you don't have a goalie, your opponents will be able to score much more easily than you. Defending the net is vital.

You know, that actually reminds me of a Bible story. Jesus is the most important person to the church, but in our story today, Paul had to take on the very important job of defending the truth of the

Younger Kids Leader Guide
Unit 30 • Session 4

gospel against false teachers who were trying to tear him down and lead people away from the truth.

Big picture question (1 minute)

LEADER • Before we get too far into the story, we need to review the big picture question and answer. Does anyone remember the question? [*Allow responses.*] That's right! ***Why does the church exist?*** How about the answer? [*Allow responses.*] Right again! ***The church exists to glorify God by worshiping Him, showing His love, and telling others about Jesus.*** That means that our purpose as believers is not to keep the good news to ourselves, but to spread it to everyone we meet. We show God's love to others and worship Him in how we live our lives.

Giant timeline (1 minute)

Show the giant timeline. Point to individual Bible stories as you review.

· Giant Timeline

LEADER • When we first started this unit, we learned that **the Holy Spirit led Philip to tell the Ethiopian man about Jesus.** Next, we learned **Jesus saved Paul and chose him to spread the gospel.** Paul planted many churches, and wrote many letters, often to the churches he planted! To the church in Colossae, Paul explained that **Jesus gives new life to people who trust in Him.** This week we will learn about what Paul wrote to the church in Corinth. The church in Corinth actually had a lot of struggles, and Paul wrote more than one letter to them. Our story today is from one of those letters to them. The story is called "Guarding the Truth."

Tell the Bible story (10 minutes)

- Bibles
- "Guarding the Truth" video
- Big Picture Question Poster
- Bible Story Picture Poster
- Story Point Poster

Open your Bible to 2 Corinthians 11. Use the Bible storytelling tips on the Bible story page to help you tell the story, or show the Bible story video "Guarding the Truth."

LEADER • Can you imagine sacrificing everything Paul had sacrificed, only to have a liar come along and try to undo the work you started? Paul was pretty upset about the false teachers. That's why he wrote the things he wrote: he didn't want anyone to lead people away from the message of salvation through faith in Jesus.

Paul wasn't writing just to defend his own reputation or to make himself look good. Paul was worried that people wouldn't live the wonderful life Jesus had for them. Paul was concerned for the church, not himself. Even when Paul used words that may have sounded like boasting, he was really just pointing people to Jesus' power. No matter what Paul suffered, he knew the gospel was worth it.

We are called to defend the truth just as Paul did. **God gives us power to stand up for the gospel.** That's why studying God's Word and gathering with the church is so important. When we do those things, along with praying, we are better equipped to defend the truth against false teachers who lead people away from Jesus.

Nowadays, false teachers may teach all kinds of things; They may say that God wants more than anything to give you lots of money and make you happy. They may say that God doesn't care about you, that God isn't the only God, or that God doesn't even exist. All of those messages are false. Only the gospel of Jesus is true. We are all sinners, and Jesus died on the cross for our sins, rising again on the third day to conquer death. Only faith in Him can save us.

Christ connection

LEADER • Sharing Jesus with the world is not always easy. There will always be some who try to stop the good news from spreading. God calls believers to follow and obey Jesus no matter what.

Questions from kids video (3 minutes)

Show the "Unit 30, Session 4" questions from kids video. Prompt kids to think about those who do not believe the Bible. Guide them to discuss how we can know the truth.

Missions moment (3 minutes)

Play the "Christian Worship Around the World" video. Discuss how different people can worship God in different ways.

LEADER • God gives people the power to stand up for the gospel, even in different countries that might not be open to the gospel. Christians around the world are worshiping Jesus in their own styles and in their own languages. Sometimes worship is not allowed by the governments, but believers are bold to gather together.

Key passage (5 minutes)

Show the key passage poster. Lead the boys and girls to read together Colossians 1:18. Then sing the key passage song.

LEADER • Jesus Christ is our greatest treasure. He deserves

Note: You may use this opportunity to use Scripture and the guide provided to explain how to become a Christian. Make sure kids know when and where they can ask questions.

· "Unit 30, Session 3" Questions from Kids video

· "Christian Worship Around the World" missions video

· Key Passage Poster
· "First Place in Everything (Colossians 1:18)" song

all the glory in our lives. That's what this verse teaches. We put Jesus first.

Sing (4 minutes)

· "One Foundation" song

LEADER • The church is one body. Paul also compares the church to buildings. A building may have a foundation of rock or stone. We have one foundation, Jesus!

Sing together "One Foundation."

Pray (2 minutes)

Invite kids to pray before dismissing to apply the story.

LEADER • Father, we know that we would be lost without You. Help us to be bold as we defend the truth from anyone who tries to lead people from Jesus. Amen.

Dismiss to apply the story

The Gospel: God's Plan for Me

Ask kids if they have ever heard the word *gospel*. Clarify that the word *gospel* means "good news." It is the message about Christ, the kingdom of God, and salvation. Use the following guide to share the gospel with kids.

God rules. Explain to kids that the Bible tells us God created everything, and He is in charge of everything. Invite a volunteer to read Genesis 1:1 from the Bible. Read Revelation 4:11 or Colossians 1:16-17 aloud and explain what these verses mean.

We sinned. Tell kids that since the time of Adam and Eve, everyone has chosen to disobey God. (Romans 3:23) The Bible calls this sin. Because God is holy, God cannot be around sin. Sin separates us from God and deserves God's punishment of death. (Romans 6:23)

God provided. Choose a child to read John 3:16 aloud. Say that God sent His Son, Jesus, the perfect solution to our sin problem, to rescue us from the punishment we deserve. It's something we, as sinners, could never earn on our own. Jesus alone saves us. Read and explain Ephesians 2:8-9.

Jesus gives. Share with kids that Jesus lived a perfect life, died on the cross for our sins, and rose again. Because Jesus gave up His life for us, we can be welcomed into God's family for eternity. This is the best gift ever! Read Romans 5:8; 2 Corinthians 5:21; or 1 Peter 3:18.

We respond. Tell kids that they can respond to Jesus. Read Romans 10:9-10,13. Review these aspects of our response: Believe in your heart that Jesus alone saves you through what He's already done on the cross. Repent, turning from self and sin to Jesus. Tell God and others that your faith is in Jesus.

Offer to talk with any child who is interested in responding to Jesus. Provide *I'm a Christian Now!* for new Christians to take home and complete with their families.

APPLY the Story

SESSION TITLE: Guarding the Truth

BIBLE PASSAGE: 2 Corinthians 11

STORY POINT: God gives us power to stand up for the gospel.

KEY PASSAGE: Colossians 1:18

BIG PICTURE QUESTION: Why does the church exist? The church exists to glorify God by worshiping Him, showing His love, and telling others about Jesus.

Key passage activity (5 minutes)

· Key Passage Poster
· permanent marker
· beach ball

Invite volunteers to say the key passage from memory. Thank each kid for his efforts and encourage all the kids to keep working to memorize the passage. Write phrases of the key passage on the sections of a beach ball. Toss the beach ball around the group for a few seconds. Every so often, say "stop." Whoever catches the ball will look at the section her right thumb is touching. She must say the verse starting from that section. Play multiple rounds.

SAY • Paul wrote many letters to believers who lived all over the Roman empire. Paul wanted to make sure they knew the truth about Jesus, the gospel, and our purpose as the church. Jesus is the head of the church; He is our leader and greatest treasure. *Why does the church exist? The church exists to glorify God by worshiping Him, showing His love, and telling others about Jesus.*

· Bibles, 1 per kid
· Story Point Poster
· Small Group Timeline and Map Set (005802970, optional)

Discussion & Bible skills (10 minutes)

Distribute a Bible to each kid. Help them find 2 Corinthians 11. Use the New Testament Mediterranean Map to point out where Corinth was located. (*D4*)

Ask the following questions. Lead the group to discuss:

1. Paul was concerned the Corinthians would be deceived just like who? (*Eve, 2 Cor. 11:3*)
2. Did Paul charge the Corinthians to share the gospel with them? (*no, 2 Cor. 11:7*)
3. What did Paul face because of his desire to share the gospel? (*all kinds of sufferings, 2 Cor. 11:23-27*)
4. Where can we find the truth about God and ourselves? *Guide kids to see that the Bible is the only source of truth about God and our relationship to Him. Lead them to discuss why we need the Bible, and how we can learn truth from it.*
5. What sufferings might we face if we stand up for the gospel? *Discuss the ways kids may feel left out or unpopular for their faith. Point out that some places in the world still face very severe persecution, such as imprisonment or even death. Remind the kids that even those severe forms of persecution cannot stop God's plan to grow the church, and that the gospel is worth facing any kind of mistreatment.*
6. Where can we get strength to face persecution and stand up for the gospel? *Remind kids that God is our source of strength. Help them see that being afraid of persecution is natural and normal. Discuss ways the Holy Spirit can help them face fears and do things that seem impossible or scary.*

SAY • **God gives us power to stand up for the gospel.** In some places, persecution may be very mild; you may only be mocked or disliked because you believe the Bible. In other places, the people may actually punish you for believing the truth. No matter what kind of persecution you face, the Holy Spirit will help you.

Option: Retell or review the Bible story using the bolded text of the Bible story script.

The Church Grew

Activity choice (10 minutes)

OPTION 1: Kids worship

· paper
· pens or pencils

Ask kids to describe their favorite part of worship. What are some of their favorite songs or things that they've seen in a worship service?

Encourage them to plan a worship service together, incorporating some of their favorite elements of worship. Remind them that all worship should be pleasing to God and should share the gospel with others. Invite them to think about Scripture reading, testimonies, music, prayer, and even an offering time.

Find a time in the near future for a special worship time for kids, allowing them to lead using their own ideas. Encourage them to invite friends. If you do not have worship for kids as a regular part of your church events, ask the staff if there is a time when one could be scheduled.

Tip: Use this activity option to reinforce the missions moment found in Teach the Story.

SAY • One day, some of you might work in churches or might be missionaries around the world. You will help others to worship God. How you choose to worship God and how you lead others to worship is an important part of missions. Worship is one way that we stand up for the gospel.

LOW PREP

OPTION 2: Stand together

Invite the class to stand side-by-side with about two feet between each kid. Challenge them to stand on one foot. You may time them to see how long they can stay standing on one foot. After the last kid loses balance, play again, allowing the kids to place hands on shoulders to hold one another steady.

SAY • **God gives us power to stand up for the gospel**.

One of the ways God gives us this power is through

the Holy Spirit, but God also gives us one another. Other believers can help you stand up for the gospel just as you can help one another stand on one foot longer.

We help one another by studying God's Word together, confessing sin to one another, encouraging one another, and meeting one another's needs.

Reflection and prayer (5 minutes)

Distribute a sheet of paper to each child. Ask the kids to write about or draw a picture to answer the following questions:

- What does this story teach me about God or about the gospel?
- What does this story teach me about myself?
- Whom can I tell about this story?

Make sure to send the sheets home with kids alongside the activity page so that parents can see what their kids have been learning.

If time remains, take prayer requests or allow kids to complete the Bible story coloring page provided with this session. Pray for your group.

· pencils and crayons
· paper
· Bible Story Coloring Page, 1 per kid

Tip: Give parents this week's Big Picture Cards for Families to allow families to interact with the biblical content at home.

Volume 1: In the Beginning

Unit 1: God Created Everything
Session 1: God Created the World *(Genesis 1)*
Session 2: God Created People *(Genesis 1–2)*
Session 3: Sin Entered the World *(Genesis 3)*
Session 4: Noah and the Ark *(Genesis 6–9)*
Session 5: The Tower of Babel *(Genesis 11)*
Session 6: The Suffering of Job *(Job)*

Unit 2: God Formed a Nation
Session 1: God's Covenant with Abraham *(Genesis 12; 15; 17)*
Session 2: Abraham and Isaac *(Genesis 22)*
Session 3: Isaac and Rebekah *(Genesis 24)*
Session 4: God's Promise to Isaac *(Genesis 25–26)*

Unit 3: The Nation Grew
Session 1: Jacob and Esau *(Genesis 27–28)*
Session 2: Jacob and Rachel *(Genesis 29–31)*
Session 3: Jacob's New Name *(Genesis 32–33)*

Volume 2: Out of Egypt

Unit 4: God's People in Egypt
Session 1: Joseph Sent to Egypt *(Genesis 37)*
Session 2: Joseph Explained Dreams *(Genesis 39–41)*
Session 3: Joseph Saved His Family *(Genesis 42–46; 50)*
Christmas: Jesus Was Born *(Isaiah 9; Luke 2)*
Session 4: Moses Was Born and Called *(Exodus 1–4)*
Session 5: The Plagues and the Passover *(Exodus 5–12)*
Session 6: The Red Sea Crossing *(Exodus 13–15)*

Unit 5: Toward the Promised Land
Session 1: Bread from Heaven *(Exodus 15–17)*
Session 2: Jethro Helped Moses *(Exodus 18)*
Session 3: The Ten Commandments *(Exodus 19–20)*

The Church Grew

Unit 12: Wise King Solomon

Volume 5: A Nation Divided

Unit 13: Elijah and Elisha

Unit 14: The Northern Kingdom of Israel

Unit 15: The Southern Kingdom of Judah

Volume 6: A People Restored

Unit 16: Hope in Exile

Unit 17: Return to the Land

Session 1: Obadiah the Prophet *(Obadiah)*
Session 2: The Captives Came Home *(Ezra 1–3)*
Session 3: The Temple Was Rebuilt *(Ezra 4–6; Haggai)*
Session 4: Zechariah the Prophet *(Zechariah)*

Unit 18: The People Restored

Session 1: Esther Saved Her People *(Esther)*
Session 2: The Walls Rebuilt *(Nehemiah 1–6)*
Session 3: God's People Repented *(Nehemiah 8–13)*
Session 4: Malachi the Prophet *(Malachi)*

Volume 7: Jesus the Messiah

Unit 19: Into the World

Session 1: From Adam to Jesus *(Matthew 1; Luke 3; John 1)*
Session 2: John Was Born *(Luke 1)*
Session 3: Jesus Was Born *(Luke 2)*
Session 4: Jesus Was Dedicated *(Luke 2)*
Session 5: Jesus as a Child *(Matthew 2; Luke 2)*

Unit 20: Prepare the Way

Session 1: Jesus' Baptism *(Matthew 3; Mark 1; Luke 3; John 1)*
Easter: Jesus' Crucifixion and Resurrection *(Matthew 26–28; 1 Corinthians 15)*
Session 2: Jesus' Temptation *(Matthew 4; Mark 1; Luke 4)*
Session 3: John Pointed to Jesus *(Matthew 3; John 1; 3)*
Session 4: Jesus Called Disciples *(Matthew 4; 9; Mark 1–3; Luke 5–6)*

Unit 21: Among the People

Session 1: Jesus' Early Miracles *(Mark 1)*
Session 2: Jesus Taught in Nazareth *(Luke 4)*
Session 3: Jesus and Nicodemus *(John 3)*
Session 4: Jesus and the Samaritan Woman *(John 4)*

Volume 8: Jesus the Servant

Unit 22: Jesus the Healer
Session 1: Jesus Healed Ten Men *(Luke 17)*
Session 2: Jesus Healed a Woman and a Girl *(Mark 5)*
Session 3: Jesus Healed a Man Who Was Lame *(John 5)*
Session 4: Jesus Healed a Man Who Was Blind *(John 9)*

Unit 23: Jesus the Teacher
Session 1: The Sermon on the Mount *(Matthew 5–7)*
Session 2: The Cost of Following Jesus *(Matthew 8; 16; Luke 9; 14)*
Session 3: Jesus Taught About Prayer *(Luke 11; 18)*
Session 4: Jesus Taught About Possessions *(Luke 12)*
Session 5: The Good Shepherd *(John 10)*

Unit 24: Jesus the Miracle-Worker
Session 1: Jesus Calmed a Storm *(Matthew 8; Mark 4; Luke 8)*
Session 2: Jesus Fed a Crowd *(Matthew 14; Mark 6; Luke 9; John 6)*
Session 3: Jesus Walked on Water *(Matthew 14; Mark 6; John 6)*
Session 4: Jesus Showed His Glory *(Matthew 17; Mark 9; Luke 9)*

Volume 9: Jesus the Savior

Unit 25: The Kingdom to Come
Session 1: Kingdom Parables *(Matthew 13)*
Session 2: Three Parables *(Luke 15)*
Session 3: Jesus' Hard Teachings *(John 6)*
Session 4: Jesus Raised Lazarus *(John 11)*

Unit 26: To the Cross
Session 1: Jesus' Triumphal Entry *(Matthew 21; Mark 11; Luke 19; John 12)*
Session 2: Jesus Was Questioned *(Matthew 22; Mark 12; Luke 20)*
Session 3: The Last Supper *(Matthew 26; Mark 14; Luke 22; John 13)*
Session 4: Jesus Was Arrested *(Matthew 26–27)*
Session 5: Jesus' Crucifixion *(Matthew 26–27; John 18–19)*

Unit 27: Out of the Grave

Session 1: Jesus' Resurrection *(Matthew 28; John 20)*
Session 2: The Emmaus Disciples *(Luke 24)*
Session 3: Jesus Appeared to the Disciples *(Luke 24; John 20)*
Session 4: Jesus Returned to Heaven *(Matthew 28; Acts 1)*

Volume 10: The Mission Begins

Unit 28: The Holy Spirit Empowers

Session 1: The Holy Spirit Came *(Acts 2)*
Session 2: Peter Healed a Man *(Acts 3–4)*
Christmas: Jesus Was Born *(John 1)*
Session 3: Faithful in Hard Times *(1 Peter 1–2)*
Session 4: Living Like Jesus *(2 Peter 1)*

Unit 29: The Early Church

Session 1: Ananias and Sapphira *(Acts 4–5)*
Session 2: Stephen's Sermon *(Acts 6–7)*
Session 3: The Good News *(Romans 5–6)*
Session 4: Doers of the Word *(James 1–2)*

Unit 30: The Church Grew

Session 1: Philip and the Ethiopian *(Acts 8)*
Session 2: Paul Met Jesus *(Acts 8–9)*
Session 3: New Life in Jesus *(Colossians 2–3)*
Session 4: Guarding the Truth *(2 Corinthians 11)*

Volume 11: The Church United

Unit 31: From Jews to Gentiles

Session 1: Peter and Cornelius *(Acts 10)*
Session 2: Barnabas in Antioch *(Acts 11)*
Session 3: Jesus Is Better *(Hebrews 1–8)*
Session 4: The Hall of Faith *(Hebrews 11)*
Easter: Jesus' Crucifixion and Resurrection *(Matthew 26–28; John 20)*

Unit 32: Making Disciples

Unit 33: A Firm Foundation

Volume 12: All Things New

Unit 34: Fight the Good Fight

Unit 35: Finishing Strong

Unit 36: Come, Lord Jesus